THE STATUS SYSTEM AND SOCIAL
ORGANIZATION OF SATSUMA

Satsuma Historical Documents Series No. 1

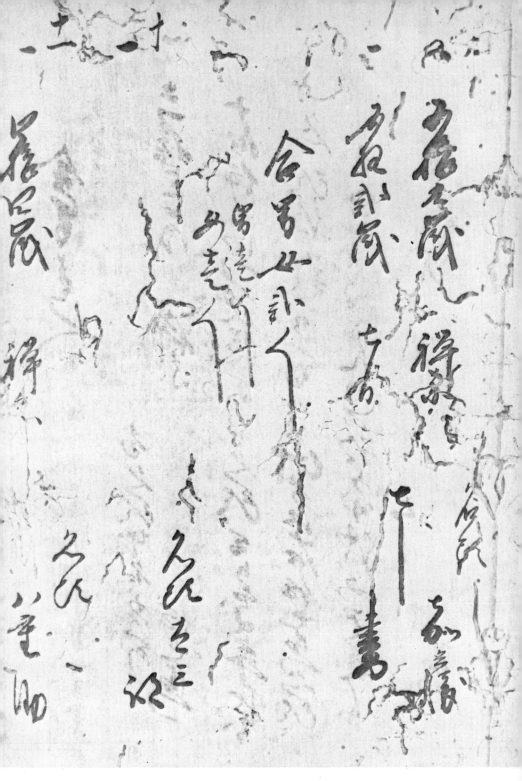

A page from the records for a preliminary (i.e., local) religious sect tag investigation. This copy is from page 9 of the record of the rural town of Yamazaki, dated the third month 1845.

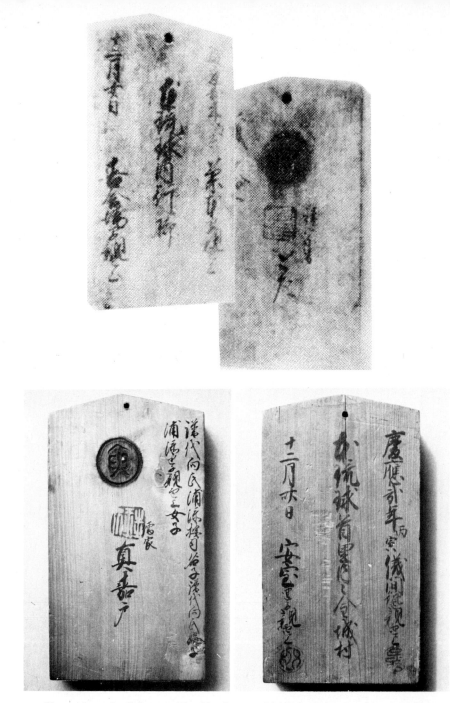

Upper photo: A religious sect identification tag which belonged to an *angya*, a wandering mendicant, of Ryukyu. Because of his quasi-outcaste status his seal was stamped sideways.

Lower photo: Shown here are religious sect identification tags from Ryukyu which are similar to those issued in Satsuma during the Tokugawa period. They are dated 12th month, 30th day, 2nd year of Keiō (1866). The size is approximately 15 cm × 8 cm × 3 cm.

These tags are now the property of the Higaonna Library, Naha, Okinawa. Photography has been obtained through the courtesy of Mr. Seisho Hokama, Chief Compiler of the History of Naha City.

THE STATUS SYSTEM
AND SOCIAL ORGANIZATION
OF SATSUMA

A translation of the *Shūmon Tefuda Aratame Jōmoku*

Analyzed and translated by

TORAO HARAGUCHI · ROBERT K. SAKAI
MITSUGU SAKIHARA · KAZUKO YAMADA
and MASATO MATSUI

with an introduction by
ROBERT K. SAKAI

THE UNIVERSITY PRESS OF HAWAII
Honolulu

Library of Congress Cataloging in Publication Data
Main entry under title:

The Status system and social organization of
Satsuma.

    English and Japanese.
    Includes bibliographical references.
    1. Religious law and legislation—Kagoshima,
Japan (Fief)—Sources. 2. Kagoshima, Japan
(Fief)—Social conditions. 3. Social status.
4. Social structure. I. Haraguchi, Torao, 1914–
Law   309.1′52′2   75-15936
ISBN 0-8248-0390-6

Dedicated to
Shunzo Sakamaki (1906–1973)
Late Dean Emeritus of the
University of Hawaii Summer Sessions

Scholar, Teacher, Administrator,
and Promotor of Asian Studies

CONTENTS

Note: The Japanese text begins at the back of the book.

ACKNOWLEDGMENTS

This volume is dedicated to the late Shunzo Sakamaki, Dean Emeritus of Summer Sessions, University of Hawaii. His untimely death occurred as the manuscript for this book was being prepared for the press. Among his many notable achievements scholars of Japanese history are especially indebted to him for his collection of the Satsuma-Ryukyu documents at the University of Hawaii. It was from this collection that the material for this volume was obtained. It was also Dean Sakamaki who made possible the organization of the translation team by bringing Professor Torao Haraguchi of the University of Kagoshima to the University of Hawaii. The members of the translation project hope that the present volume to some extent approaches the expectations which he had of our endeavor.

The production of this book was by team effort. Professor Haraguchi conducted a seminar for the other members of the group, bringing to bear his special expertise in Satsuma documents by providing the correct readings for the difficult pre-Meiji script, suggesting punctuation points for the original text, and explicating terms and phrases which in many cases are peculiar to Satsuma. The other members of the team then undertook the translation of the text into English, a difficult task because the original text was not always clear. Daily sessions of a few hours each were held for several months, hammering out differences of interpretation, tracing the internal logic of the document, and checking the translation by content analysis. The translation underwent several revisions, but no doubt there is still room for varying interpretations. The translators themselves are not in complete agreement on all points, but it was decided that, while over-translation should be avoided, definite positions should be taken on interpretations wherever possible, especially since the reader can refer to the Japanese text. Comments and suggestions from readers, therefore, will be welcomes.

It is hoped that this book will be useful for different categories of readers. For those who do not read Japanese the translation provides an astounding view of a segment of Tokugawa society. For those who wish to acquire competency in the reading of premodern historical documents the Japanese text and the translation together will serve as an introduction. Japanese terms which appear in the translated text or in the introductory essay are explained briefly in the appended Glossary. The essay is intended to suggest ways of organizing or interpreting the data.

Mrs. Kazuko Yamada assumed the primary responsibility for transcribing the Japanese text from *sōsho* script into *kaisho*. She has also added the punctuation marks which are absent from the original text, but which are important for the proper understanding of the text. Dr. Mitsugu Sakihara had charge of coordinating, organizing, and preparing the final draft of the glossary. The Introductory Analysis was written by Professor Robert K. Sakai.

It should be noted also that in the original Japanese text the chapters and articles were not numbered. Sequential numbers were added both in the translated text and in the present Japanese text.

The editors and translators are grateful for the support services which were provided by the staffs of the Summer Sessions Office, the History Department, and the Social Science Research Institute of the University of Hawaii. Mrs. Sady Sakai and Mrs. Freda Hellinger helped us avoid stylistic errors and prepared the preliminary and the final draft copies. We also wish to extend our appreciation to the editorial staff of the University of Tokyo Press, from whom we have received much encouragement and cooperation.

THE STATUS SYSTEM AND SOCIAL
ORGANIZATION OF SATSUMA

Part 1
AN INTRODUCTORY ANALYSIS

AN INTRODUCTORY ANALYSIS

ROBERT K. SAKAI

The *Shūmon tefuda aratame jōmoku* ("Regulations for the Investigation of Religious Sects and Identification Tags") richly details the social organization and status system of Satsuma in the midnineteenth century. The document provides us a close view of the social structure of traditional Japan, and at the same time the description of social relations gives clues as to the basis of political strength and leadership which enabled Satsuma to play the leading role in the Restoration Movement.

In the following pages we shall refer to the *Shūmon tefuda aratame jōmoku* simply as the *Jōmoku*, or *Regulations*. These regulations were updated and reissued by the *han* government from time to time. The present translation is of an edition officially copied in the first month of the fifth year of Kaei (1852). Included in this edition are some regulations which were originally decreed in the early seventeenth century. This particular edition of the *Jōmoku* provides us especially with the official attitudes and policies on social organization and status over the period of the century immediately preceding the arrival of Commodore Matthew C. Perry to Japan.

As the title indicates, the regulations were initially formulated for the purpose of enforcing the country-wide anti-Christian edicts promulgated by the Tokugawa Bakufu early in the seventeenth century. Everyone in Japan was required to register at his local temple and declare his faith. Furthermore, each person was issued

5

a wooden identification tag which he was required to wear at all times. This proscription act, onerous for the people at that time, resulted in a legacy of documents which contemporary scholars have found valuable for population studies.

In the case of Satsuma, however, the records are especially detailed. This was due to the fact that unlike the practice in other *han,* the registration and investigation procedures were entrusted to the civil administrators of the domain. By directly controlling the registration process, instead of relegating the responsibility to temples, Satsuma was able to extend the religious ban to include the Ikkō sect of Buddhism and to broaden the intent from religious control to general social control. Detailed information about the social background of every man, woman, and child in the *han* was submitted, verified, and entered into the register, thereby officially fixing the individual's place in society and his obligations and prerogatives. A quick glance through the *Jōmoku* makes readily apparent that by the early nineteenth century religious proscription had become a minor part of a major policy for social control. In fact, the Bakufu's anti-Christian edict is given only perfunctory mention, though detailed attention is given to Satsuma's anti-Ikkō program.

Why the Ikkō sect was persecuted in Satsuma is not entirely clear, but official hostility predated the beginning of the Tokugawa period. Continued existence of this sect, in defiance of the ban, however, resulted in renewed efforts at suppression and the development of a sophisticated investigative and control procedure. Travel was severely restricted; wandering priests and minstrels were placed under surveillance; and identification tags not only noted the bearer's present religious affiliation, but also, if he had recanted, his dubious status as "former Ikkō believer." Between 1635 (when the first *han*-wide investigation was carried out, a process which required four years to complete) and 1700, investigations were carried out irregularly with intervals of three to twelve years. Between 1700 and 1761 the intervals were seven to eight years. The next period from 1761 to 1824 was somewhat more relaxed with five domain investigations spaced erratically and far between. After 1824, however, an official investigation was carried out throughout Satsuma every seven years. Moreover, after 1796 two district officials (*shūmon kata kakari*) charged with responsibility for checking sectarian membership, circulated among the villagers two or three times a year, and semi-annually (fifth and twelfth months) local community heads gathered the people together to remind them of the government injunctions.[1] The instructions for registration were compiled in the *Shūmon tefuda aratame jōmoku*, which in its later form became an instrument for virtually totalitarian population control.

Obviously, the scholar must exercise caution in using this document. One cannot conclude that all the regulations were equally enforced. Regulations reflect the intentions of the regulators, and often it is difficult to evaluate the degree of compliance by the regulated. Sometimes one may detect a note of urgency in the official language, which suggests that hitherto people had not adhered to particular rules. One may also note the repetitious use of certain phrases which had become bureaucratic jargon, perhaps devoid of literal significance.

Nevertheless, the regulations do give us amazing detail about the official rules, how they were to be carried out, and who were responsible for checking on them. The exceptionally large bureaucratic staff which penetrated down to the lowest social unit of the village,[2] the system of joint responsibility through Satsuma's unique system of household collectives based on land allotments (the *kadowari seido*), and the elaborate provisions for checks and counterchecks do give us some assurance that there was a meaningful correlation between the regulations and social reality. The fact that the regulations were frequently revised and brought up to date suggests that the government was anxious to make the laws realistic and viable.

---

[1] Momozono Keishin, "Sappan ni okeru shūmoɪ tefuda aratame no jisshi kaisū ni tsuite," *Kadai Shigaku*, No. 2 (1954), pp. 27–33.
[2] Satsuma's ratio of samurai to commoner, nearly 1:3, was the highest in the country. These samurai constituted the reservoir for the *han* bureaucracy. This domain was unique in that samurai were placed in charge of villages in the countryside whereas in other areas a measure of local autonomy was the general rule.

1. The Overview of Satsuma Socity: Status and Functional Differentiations

As in other parts of Japan in the Tokugawa period, Satsuma society was divided into two broad categories, the privileged upper class and the commoner class. The former was ranked by status and the latter was divided into separate communities on a functional basis. The official perspective on social differentiation in Satsuma is reflected in the chapter titles of the *Jōmoku*. There are twenty-four chapters, some long and some very brief. The chapters indicate which groups of people belonged to particular social categories or functional units. From this, one may deduce the official rationale for social classifications. The sequence of titles provides further clues concerning the social hierarchy; generally the arrangement begins with the highest rank (chapter II) and concludes with the outcaste groups (chapter XXIV).

The privileged class, i.e., people with surnames, their equivalents in the religious establishments, and their dependents, are the subject of chapters II to XI. Important families have large households with retainers and domestic dependents. The latter are treated in the same chapters with their samurai masters as well as in separate sections. This inclusion of dependents and retainers suggests that the household, rather than the nuclear family, was regarded by the authorities as the basic social unit, particularly among the upper social ranks. The fact that the chapter on *gōshi* (rural samurai) is placed ahead of the discussion of subretainers and servants of *jōkashi* (castle-town samurai) reflects the official bias in terms of the prestige factor.

The functional communities are treated in chapters XII through XVI. There were four basic types of rural villages: religious settlements, agricultural villages, rural towns, and fishing communities. In addition there were towns and special communities. The title of the immediate administrative supervisor for each of these types was distinctive. Since these communities are divided in accordance with their economic activities and obligations, probably we should not give much emphasis to the sequence in which they are discussed. Nevertheless it is intriguing that Naishirogawa, a settlement of Korean potters, is high on this list, preceding even the chapter on the townsmen of the castle-town (Kagoshima).

Chapters XVII through XX deal with individuals or families who for various reasons are located away from their *han* or from their basic families, households, or villages. Some are officially employed outside of the domain; others are *rōnin,* runaways, exiles, and others who have violated the regulations or in other ways incurred the daimyo's displeasure. Special regulations were necessary to cover these individuals, since normally everyone was expected to be attached to, or be the responsibility of, legally recognized social units such as households, samurai units, religious institutions, or village communities.

Irregularities concerning the maintenance of the identification tags, false information or procedural errors, and their respective fines and punishments are the concern of chapters XXI and XXII. The final two chapters are of interest, not only for their content, but also because of their sequence. Instead of placing the chapter entitled "Miscellaneous" at the very end, it is placed ahead of the discussion of *kengo,* and *eta* (outcaste groups) and *angya* (wandering mendicants). Apparently in status-conscious Satsuma these outcaste groups necessarily must be put in last place.

The samurai relationship to the daimyo

Studies of the Meiji Restoration Movement have led many scholars to inquire about the social origins of the Restoration leaders, but a particularly difficult problem has been that of demarcating upper, middle, and lower rank samurai. One seemingly rational solution to this puzzle has been to apply an economic standard, i.e., ascertaining the rice income of the samurai and establishing somewhat arbitrary figures to denote those above the figure to middle rank and those below the figure to be lower rank, etc. The income factor is convenient as an inflexible and impersonal yard-stick, but it is also inaccurate for the same reason. While income was one measure of a man's rank and status, the ethical bias of the samurai was to deemphasize the economic factor as a measure of one's dignity and social value.

There was intense consciousness of social status in Satsuma. This phenomenon strikes the reader most forcefully in perusing the *Jōmoku*. Regardless of financial situation it was the proper recognition of their social position by others which was the critical factor for most samurai. Witness, for example, the poignant plea of the thirty-five retainers of Shimazu Buzen who requested and obtained identification as members of "Hishida Group, Miyakonojō" to avoid being mistaken for fishermen [ch. II. 2]. Interestingly, in this document, which emphasizes the proper definition of each person's social station, the correlation with income is infrequent. It is probable, therefore, that classification of samurai by income is a methodological convenience which does not necessarily correspond to the contemporary understanding of one's social identification and importance.

Status in Satsuma was codified by official regulations, ritualized in terms of the status holder's relationship to the daimyo, and verified by periodic investigations. Among the upper ranks of samurai there were two categories, those with *dokurei* privilege and those with *chakuza* privilege. *Dokurei* status meant that the individual in this position was privileged to have a private audience with the daimyo on the first day of the year and the first day of the eighth month. A person of *chakuza* status was one who was assigned a seat in the audience chamber where together with his peers he was privileged to greet the daimyo on these two auspicious days.

Among those of *dokurei* status [see ch. II] the most prestigious were the *ichimon* families. These were the four main branch families (legally so designated) of the daimyo, each bearing the Shimazu surname. They served the daimyo in much the same way as the *gosanke* who counselled the Tokugawa shogun.[3] In addition there were four other Shimazu families of *isshomochi* rank who were elevated above their peers by virtue of their *dokurei* privilege. Frequently a ninth family was included in this illustrious group, that of the lord of Tanegashima, from whence the daimyo often selected his consort. In addition to these kin relations of the daimyo, others grouped with the most prestigious were the highest officials of the

[3]Kagoshima-ken, ed. and pub., *Kagoshima kenshi* (Tokyo, 1940), 2:19.

domain with bureaucratic posts of *ōmetsuke* and above, plus the baronial vassals who held private territory with an income assessment of 10,000 *koku* or more.

The *chakuza* group constituting the second highest social category included the households of the ranks of *isshomochi, isshomochi-kaku, yoriai,* and *yoriai-nami*. The first title implied that the title-holder possessed and had jurisdiction over an entire administrative district; the second title denoted a person of almost equivalent rank with the first, though without the lordship over a district; the third title suggests that the rank initially corresponded to that of commander; and the fourth was but slightly lower in social standing than the third.

The *dokurei* and *chakuza* groups monopolized all of the chief administrative posts in the *han* bureaucracy. They each had large households and many retainers, and the *kokudaka* (rice income) was commensurately high. Although the hereditary principle was important, the inheritance of status was not to be taken for granted. It had to be verified and officially recognized by entry into the register and ritualized by protocol governing the individual's relationship to the daimyo.

The *chakuza* and *dokurei* privileges provided the means by which the social ranking of each person of high status could be fixed exactly. We may assume that on ceremonial days when officials made their calls on the daimyo, those of *dokurei* status met in turn with the *han* lord according to well-defined sequence. According to the *Jōmoku* [ch. II. 24], when the lord of Tanegashima was granted *dokurei* status, he was granted "a rank next to that of *ichimon* and at the top of the [*isshomochi*] rank held by Shimazu Wakasa and his peers." The exactness of definition of rank and ceremonial seating order may be surmised by studying Chapter VI of the *Jōmoku,* wherein the protocol for *chakuza* priests is set forth in minute detail.

In a society such as Satsuma, where social prestige and status played such an important role in the proper ordering of the *han* state, it was desirable, if not essential, to have a single ranking system. Thus it was logical that the religious establishments, like the prestigious samurai families, were ranked in terms of their importance to the daimyo and accorded corresponding privileges. This procedure permitted easy status identification of heads of these establishments in terms of their samurai counterparts with whom marriage ties were permitted. Even the titles of the dependents of religious establishments were the same as for those in samurai households [e.g., ch. VI. 13].

Status for the individual cleric derived from his position within the religious establishment, however, and upon his separation from his temple or shrine he also was separated from his high status. In other words, status was assigned to the religious establishment, not to the individual. Although important positions in the most prestigious temples and shrines generally were filled by members of high-ranking samurai, it was possible in some instances for commoners to attain to the top religious post by dint of hard study. In such an event a person of low birth would be on social parity with some of the more powerful samurai of the domain.

In the third highest level in the social hierarchy of Satsuma below the *dokurei* and *chakuza,* were the samurai who were collectively called *jōkashi* or *shoshi* ("castle-town samurai"). There were three ranks in this group, the *koban, shimban* and *koshōgumi.* The *koban* often were cadet families of the most prestigious households. Likewise the *shimban* ("new guards") rank was created to take care of certain sons of the second level of samurai.[4] The *koban* samurai especially were prestigious, but not enough to warrant a direct formal relationship with the *han* lord. The *koban* (literally "small guard") were a rather elite group entrusted with the security of the inner grounds of the daimyo residence. In making their rounds they were privileged to ride on horses.

Members of this third social group were warrior retainers of the daimyo. As such they reported their marriages to the *han* lord. It is not clear from the *Jōmoku* whether all marriages in this category were required to be reported, but the formality probably was the critical one in separating the full-fledged castle-town samurai from those whose status limited them to functional roles which did not carry the prestige of the fighter-administrator. Within this third group some were permitted to submit gifts to the daimyo and others were not. The level of gift giving was defined further in terms of the individual's standing within the family. Probably the submission of gifts to the *han* lord was limited to those of *koban* rank and higher.

d., 2:23.

Social mobility among Satsuma samurai

Social mobility in Satsuma, as in other areas of Japan in the Tokugawa period, was conditioned by the relatively rigid pyramid-shaped social hierarchy. There was movement, however, both upward and downward within the structure. Naturally it was easier to lose status than to gain status, for the higher positions were legally limited and restricted. Moreover, the regulations specified which members of the family were permitted to enjoy the privileges associated with the high position of the household head. Younger sons for whom there were no prestigious titles were relegated to lower ranks, such as *koban* and *shimban*. The *han* lord sometimes decreed a sudden drop in status. The *Jōmoku* also provides us with the interesting cases of Kameyama Isamu and Yamada Shozō, who in 1786 were ordered to be "without rank" (*mukaku*). [See ch. V.] It is not clear which rank they had previously occupied, but the fact that their maids were to be designated "*tsukai-onna*" suggests that they were demoted to a status below that of the *koban*, whose maids were registered as "*naijo*."

Among the castle-town samurai (*jōkashi*) those in the *koban* rank were the highest, and below them were the thousands of rank-and-file samurai of *shimban* and *koshōgumi* ranks. Many in the *koban* rank were of distinguished lineage and had influential connections, and we may assume that occasionally they received promotions in status or assignments to positions generally reserved for people high in the social hierarchy. The *Jōmoku* [ch. IV. 1] refers to people "who are not of *yoriai-nami* rank or higher, but who serve as commander of the outer guards, magistrate of temples and shrines, magistrate of accounting, captain of *koshōgumi* guard unit, or chief duty officer. . . ." These people undoubtedly came from the *koban* rank, and since the appointments were for one generation, when the official left his post he and his household reverted to their permanent hereditary status.

Similarly, samurai of *shimban* and *koshōgumi* ranks might be given *koban* status if they served in important positions such as magistrate of guns. In these cases the *koban* status was for one generation only, and the maids of such samurai were registered as "*tsukai-onna*" rather than "*naijo*," a term reserved for female servants in a *koban* or higher household [ch. IV. 2]. Temporary status promotion was a convenient device for utilizing the administrative talents of lower-ranking Satsuma samurai.

One other example may be cited to illustrate the possibilities and limitations of social mobility within the social structure of Satsuma samurai. According to the regulations, a *gōshi* (rural samurai) may not be adopted by a *koban* rank samurai, but when such becomes necessary the latter is demoted to the status of *koshōgumi* [ch. VIII. 2]. In this case the status of the adopted son certainly improves from *gōshi* to *koshōgumi*, but that of the adopting parent drastically declines. This rule guarded against a too liberal adoption system which would devalue the status system.

Gōshi and quasi-samurai

Below the *koshōgumi*, the bottom rank of the *jōkashi* ("castle-town samurai") category, there were two other groups, usually described as samurai, but who were less well-defined in terms of their social position. These were, first, the *gōshi* ("rural samurai") and the *shiryōshi* (subretainers of powerful vassals of the *han* lord); second, the *yoriki, ashigaru,* and various other individuals of miscellaneous titles which usually denoted their functional duties. These somewhat inchoate groups pose particular difficulties for historians who seek to establish exactly the social origins of individuals along class lines.

Some scholars refer to the *koshōgumi* samurai as low rank and others refer to them as middle rank. In terms of the particular methodological approach, which emphasizes class confrontation as a dynamic factor in the process of history, the distinction between low and middle is crucial. It is Satsuma's *koshōgumi* rank that produced some of the outstanding national leaders of modern Japan, such as Saigō Takamori and Ōkubo Toshimichi. Were their class origins low or middle rank?

The problem derives from the fact that Satsuma's official views, as reflected in the *Jōmoku,* were not concerned with the methodological problems of later historians. The official concern was to define the social positions and feudal obligations of different types of people vis-à-vis the daimyo. Basically the Satsuma authorities viewed the total *han* society along a vertical axis, the *han* lord being at one end and the different levels of people extending along its length toward the other.

Exactness in correspondence to an abstract concept of "lowness" or "middleness" of a rank was not as important as the relative position of one rank to another and the obligations to the daimyo pertaining to each. It was important for the *koshōgumi* samurai, for example, to know precisely who were his superiors and inferiors; his problem was not "am I middle rank or low rank?" There was no question in his mind that *gōshi* and their rural counterparts, the subretainers of vassals, were not as prestigious as he. As a castle-town samurai he was directly at the service of the daimyo, whereas his country cousins were geographically and psychologically farther removed from their lord.

Returning to the problem of contemporary scholars, however, if the *koshōgumi* samurai was at the bottom rung of the samurai ladder, then many *gōshi* and subretainers, and most, if not all, *yoriki, ashigaru,* and other lesser individuals should not be regarded as samurai, despite references to them in the documents as *shi,* or "samurai." On the other hand, if these latter groups are indeed samurai then the *koshōgumi* must be described as middle rank.

I would suggest that the inherent logic of the *Jōmoku* was to emphasize status differentiation for the samurai class and functional differentiation for the common people. Using this standard we can point to generic characteristics of samurai (and their equivalents) as distinct from those of non-samurai. The *koshōgumi* samurai had a direct and personal relationship to the daimyo, as reflected in his obligation to notify the lord concerning his marriage. His life was dedicated to service to his lord in peace or in war, as administrator or as soldier. Thus he considered himself a social elite, wearing two swords and brooking no insult from lesser creatures.

Among the so-called samurai who were lower than *koshōgumi,* emphasis on status diminished and function was emphasized. Thus there was an in-between group in Satsuma, some of the members properly belonging to the samurai category and others of whom may be described as quasi-samurai. These will be discussed in turn.

For purposes of analysis it is convenient to deal with the *gōshi* and those of the subretainers who resided in the countryside as one group, although the former regarded himself to be socially better than the latter. The attitude stems from the fact that the *gōshi* considered himself to be a retainer of the daimyo, while the sub-retainer owed his allegiance to his liege lord, who was a vassal of the daimyo. Both *gōshi* and their subretainer counterparts concentrated in rural communities of their peers. The *gōshi* gen-erally were concentrated in communities called *gōjū*, located at each district seat; and the subretainers also were grouped together at the seat of their local administrative unit, the *shiryō* ("private ter-ritory" of the vassal). The district and *shiryō* were roughly equiva-lent units, one being supervised by the *jitō*, an upper rank official in the castle-town, and the other by the territorial holder, also re-siding in Kagoshima.

Gōshi were originally the equal of the *koshōgumi* samurai. Gradu-ally their status had been denigrated, and, as can be seen in the *Jōmoku,* during the latter part of the Tokugawa period many were permitted to marry commoners. Among the *gōshi* there was a wide disparity of status between those who were full-time district administrators and those who were primarily occupied with self-sustenance through agriculture. There was little to differentiate the latter from the peasants. In between the extremes were *gōshi* who served as minor officials, clerks, village heads, and guards. Cer-tainly the more important *gōshi* officials should be ranked along with the *koshōgumi,* though not with the *koban* rank, for the regula-tions prohibit *gōshi* daughters and sons from marriage to and adop-tion by the *koban* samurai.

On the other hand, a majority of the *gōshi* were more like peas-ants than samurai. The *jōkashi* (castle-town samurai) certainly looked down on them as rustics. It was a saying among them that for a *gōshi* a sheet of paper sufficed, meaning that only a brief apology and explanation were necessary to exonerate a castle-town samurai for his killing a *gōshi*. To be sure, the latter were the ele-ment in Satsuma's unique system which enabled the *han* govern-ment to maintain such thorough control over the entire rural population and to enforce its own seclusion policy, which kept out strangers and prevented unauthorized departures from the domain. *Gōshi* were in charge of every peasant village, fishing community, and rural town, and they served as guards at strategic barriers and highway checkpoints. The government thus valued their services, but for the maintenance of these services the authorities were willing to water down their social status or to elevate that of some local commoners who supplemented the *gōshi* manpower. In cases where their services seemed to be threatened by a shrinking population the remedy was to permit *gōshi* marriages with commoners in the immediate area.

The thinness of the line between *gōshi* and commoner is attested also by the regulation which refers to demotions of *gōshi* to *meshitsukai* ("servant") status. When that happened the former *gōshi* was not much better than a servant of peasant origin, for the two are lumped together in the *Jōmoku* [ch. XV. 16].

It must be concluded that from both the official and popular points of view, though perhaps not in terms of the *gōshi*'s own self-esteem, the social status of rural warriors had deteriorated. The trend was for the poorer *gōshi* to become less distinct from the common people and further removed from their former peer group, the *jōkashi*. Most of the *gōshi* of Satsuma, therefore, could be classified as no better than quasi-samurai.

A second large group ranking below the *koshōgumi* was composed of *yoriki, ashigaru,* and their equivalents. People in these ranks usually bore surnames, but they were not required to report their marriages to the daimyo. By the same token they were not permitted to marry those who did report to the lord. This distinction emphasizes the different relationship of each to the *han* lord.

From the point of view of the *han* lord the *yoriki* and *ashigaru* were important for their manual skills and personal services. They were not associated with the samurai unit, *kumi,* but were attached to *za,* which were offices providing particular skills and services. The *yoriki*'s immediate supervisor [*shihaigashira*] not only directed his work, he also assumed responsibility for the *yoriki*'s well-being and good conduct, vouching for the accuracy of the latter's entries in the registration process. The regulations were more concerned with the *yoriki*'s function than with the preservation of his status.

From the regulations we may infer that the *yoriki* and *gōshi* were on relatively equal social standing, slightly above that of the *ashigaru*. One-generation appointments are mentioned in the *Jō-moku* for both *gōshi* [ch. X. 12] and *yoriki* [ch. IX. 1] ranks. In the latter case the appointment was officially justified by the *goyōnin*, an important *han* official in charge of economic matters. This suggests that the one-generation *yoriki* was selected probably from among the *ashigaru,* thus placing him above the latter. The social position of the *yoriki* is suggested by the phrase which permitted him to marry a person "whose status does not permit marriage with a castle-town samurai" [ch. IX. 3] and by the prohibition of *shozatsuki* (the commoners attached to the various offices) from marrying castle-town samurai, *gōshi,* and *yoriki* [ch. IX. 11]. The *yoriki* and *gōshi,* according to this, are almost, but not quite, like the castle-town samurai. Their daughters were not allowed to marry samurai who must report their marriages to the daimyo [ch. IX. 4]. Moreover, when a one-generation-*yoriki* died, his family reverted to *ashigaru* status [ch. IX. 4].

The *ashigaru* was a general category of menials performing tasks for the *han* and for samurai of higher status. The regulations [ch. IX. 6] equate the *ashigaru* with the daimyo's grooms, messengers, and tea servers, each of whom was permitted the use of a surname. The difference between the *ashigaru* and the *koshōgumi* obviously was great. To refer to *ashigaru* as low-ranking samurai is to confuse the meaning of the term. Thus, as in the case of most *gōshi,* the term "quasi-samurai" may be more appropriate.

To summarize this discussion of upper-class status, we may say that the *Jōmoku* and the registration process established clear distinctions between the samurai of castle-town status and those of lower rank. We have mentioned the marriage taboo between those who reported their marriages to the daimyo and those who did not. Perhaps an even more basic distinction is made by the *Jōmoku* by its strict regulation of samurai status on the one hand and the quasi-samurai's function on the other. As the prime defender of the daimyo's authority the samurai's honor and prestige were clearly defined. The positions of *yoriki* and *ashigaru* were generically different, for they did not control other people's lives; they were not direct extensions of the daimyo's civil and military arms. Instead they were valued for performance of specific functions. For the samurai, status was almost their raison d'être; for the *yoriki* and *ashigaru* it was a secondary consideration, in a sense, a recognition of their support in the military-civil system. The following analysis of the regulations governing the registration of commoners brings out even more clearly the contrasting emphasis on status and function.

The functional basis for corporate villages

Two principles governed the organization of villages in Satsuma: (1) Each rural community was legally classified according to its economic activity and (2) each community had legal obligations to carry out specific services for the daimyo (the latter term, in effect, meaning his government).

There were several categories of rural settlements. We have already mentioned the *gōjū*, which were communities for *gōshi*. Although *gōshi* were not commoners, their communities were in rural districts. The *gōjū* were located in the district administrative centers, which were formerly called *tojō*, or "outer castles," reflecting the earlier system of military-political organization of the *han*. Satsuma was unique in Tokugawa Japan because of her *tojō* system. Even though the former castles were destroyed, the administrative centers and the disposition of rural warriors remained even into the mid-nineteenth century. The *gōshi* in these centers served to oversee the activities of the commoners and enforce the regulations emanating from Kagoshima, the main castle-town.

A second type of rural settlement was the *zaigō*. This was the agricultural village composed of *hyakushō* (peasants, or agriculturists). A unique feature of Satsuma village organization was the *kadowari seido* ("*kado* allotment system"), a *kado* being a collective of households. Each village was divided into *kado* subunits. The main household of the *kado* was headed by the *myōzu,* and the heads of dependent households within the *kado* were called *nago*. Each household in the *kado* was responsible for an allotment of land. However, these peasants did not receive full title to the land, only the right and obligation to cultivate it. Members of the *kado* were jointly responsible for submitting the annual rice tax to the government as well as for providing a month of labor service each year. Joint responsibility, in effect, meant that the *kado* was a mechanism for self-enforcement of *han* laws.

A third category of rural settlement was called *nomachi*, or "rural town." It was not a *machi*, or "town," in the usually accepted sense of the word. The *nomachi* was a very small community in which a few merchants carried on a limited trade of essential commodities not locally available to an otherwise self-sufficient rural population. These merchants also rendered services to the local agents of the daimyo, i.e., the *gōshi*, and they maintained rest facilities and coolie services for official travellers, including the daimyo and his retinue en route to or on his return from Edo. Except for these occasional services and minor commercial activities, the life of the rural merchant and his family was not too different from that of the peasant. Thus it is not surprising that in the *Jōmoku* the regulations for the *nomachi* are couched in the same chapter as for the *zaigō*. In any case, these residents were not the thriving rural commercial entrepreneurs found in certain other parts of Japan.

A fourth type of rural settlement was the *ura* or *hama* (coastal or fishing villages), which subsisted basically on the products of the sea and by maritime activities. There were many of these communities along the well-indented coastline and river mouths of Satsuma. Their obligation to the *han* was to provide boats and laborers for ferry service or ship and crew for transporting officials and commodities for longer journeys. Many engaged in inter-*han* trade, others were licensed to engage in the Satsuma-Ryukyu trade, and still others flourished from the littoral smuggling traffic. The *ura* and *hama* residents were a valuable asset for the *han* economy.

A fifth category of rural settlements was attached to religious establishments. These communities were called *teramonzen*, or "temple-gate" settlements. Temple-gate residents engaged in various activities such as setting up shops during religious festivals, tapping the pilgrim trade, farming, or fishing. Their primary activity was to provide economic support for their respective religious establishments, but they also had public labor services to fulfill.

There were other special communities identified in the *Jōmoku*, such as Naishirogawa (a community of Korean hereditary potters), mining communities, and communities for the social outcastes. There were also mixed communities, called *han-ura*, which were part agricultural and part fishing in their functional obligations.

A major reason for the classification of villages was to fix their corporate obligations to the *han*. Local officials were assigned to oversee the fulfillment of these obligations. For the *zaigō, nomachi,* and *ura* or *hamamachi* the headmen were the *shōya, bettō,* and *ura yakunin* respectively. In fact, it can be said that the title of the official in charge of the village indicated the functional classification of that settlement. It is significant that in each case the village headman was a *gōshi*, not a commoner resident in the community. This is evidence of the lack of village autonomy in Satsuma in contrast to the situation in other parts of Japan. Above the village level, the administrative official for the *zaigō* and *nomachi* was the magistrate of agriculture [*kōri bugyō*] or the agricultural overseer [*kōrimimai*], while for the fishing villages there was the maritime magistrate [*funa bugyō*]. Occasionally there was difficulty in determining the proper classification of a village. For example, Nayamachi and Tōkamachi in Chōsa district had become semi-fishing villages with characteristics of the *nomachi* [ch. XVI. 30, 32]. The former remained under the administrative jurisdiction of the magistrate of agriculture and the latter under the maritime magistrate.

The *teramonzen*, or temple-gate settlements, were administered by the magistrate for temples and shrines [*jisha bugyō*], while the mining communities were under the jurisdiction of the magistrate for gold mines [*kinzan bugyō*]. The *Jōmoku* does not mention the title of the magistrate for either the community of Korean potters in Naishirogawa, or for the settlements of social outcastes. Presumably the communities were under the jurisdiction of the *kōri bugyō*.

It is convenient to mention at this point that in addition to the rural settlements there were commoners also in urban *machi*, or "towns." There were three (Kamimachi, Shimomachi, and Nishidamachi) located within the castle-town of Kagoshima. These were merchant districts; the residents of these *machi* provided goods and services for the city and government. Some were influential merchants with licenses which gave them monopoly rights to certain transactions. The privileged merchants were sometimes granted quasi-samurai status as *hitokerai* which entitled them to the use of surname and to arrange marriages with others having similar quasi-samurai status.

2. Economic Functions and Marriage Relationships

Whereas marriages among the privileged class were arranged between people of similar status, marriages for the common people were governed by functions. As a rule peasants, rural townspeople, and fishing villagers married people within their own villages or with villagers from other *zaigō*, *nomachi*, or *ura* respectively. Since the *Jōmoku* [ch. XV. 36] states that residents of these three types of communities were all in the same non-samurai category, and hence ineligible to have surnames except in special cases, status was not of primary importance. Marriage restrictions were established for commoners to match people of similar economic functions and responsibilities. The government was determined that the various types of functional villages should maintain a level of population adequate to fulfill their public services. This required a population control policy which involved regulating marriages and adoption.

Satsuma's marriage regulations for commoners were pragmatic and adjustable to changing situations. For example, the residents of Naishirogawa were Koreans by racial origin. They were highly skilled potters and thus valuable to the *han*. The regulations provided that these potters should be allowed to bring in outsiders for purposes of matrimony, but residents were not permitted to leave the village to join families in other communities [ch. XIII. 2]. Such a distinction was designed to protect the pottery industry by preventing a population outflow. Similarly, residents of the *nomachi* could marry their daughters to villagers of the *zaigō*, but daughters of peasants were not permitted marriage into a *nomachi* community [ch. XV. 13]. This regulations reflected the official value placed on agricultural production; the functions of the *no-machi* were relatively limited and did not require a large population.

The functional basis for regulating marriages is most clearly stated in the following:

> Proviso: Marriage reciprocity shall be permitted among townsmen who reside in the above three town districts [i.e., the three *machi* of the castle-town, Kamimachi, Shimomachi, and Nishidamachi], fishing villagers who are under the supervision of the two maritime magistrates, and temple-gate personnel of Nansen'in and Nanrinji and of the temples of Daijiji, Kaitokuji, and Eitaiji in Shibushi district, because these people provide maritime corvée service. Others who do not provide such service shall not be permitted the above type of marriage relationship [ch. XIV. 4; also ch. XVI. 15].

In the above three types of communities, the urban *machi*, the *ura* and *hama* (under the jurisdiction of the maritime magistrate), and certain of the temple-gate settlements were permitted reciprocal marriage relationships because each was located by the sea and served the daimyo in providing water transportation.

People who had access to the sea, and hence had greater mobility along the coast, often were allowed wider opportunities for establishing marital ties than those whose responsibilities were to till the land. Generally the regulations limited the range of marriage relationships to a single district (*gō*) or to neighboring districts. The reasons for setting geographical limits to the marriage network is not clear. Economic (cost) and administrative (convenience) factors probably entered in.

One may note that in chapter XV of the *Jōmoku*, which deals with the *zaigō* and *nomachi* popuiations, there is virtually no mention of petitions from the peasant population in the *zaigō* requesting modification of the above general rules. Apparently the farm villages were sufficiently stable and the population balance was satisfactory, so that petitions for setting aside marriage rules were not necessary. The absence of such peasant petitions is in sharp contrast to the many requests submitted by the *nomachi*.

Although the general rule prohibited peasant brides from joining rural townsmen, this seems to have been set aside easily. The *Jōmoku* makes reference to some fifty-nine rural towns located in fifty-five different districts.[5] Of the fifty-nine *nomachi* fifty-six are recorded as having petitioned for permission to marry peasants or other commoners within the district or within two or more neighboring districts. The petitions were granted in each case.

There are some obvious reasons for such petitions. First, there were few rural towns in Satsuma and these were well scattered. Normally there was no more than one *nomachi* per district, but about half of the total number of 113 districts did not have any *nomachi*. Distance made inter-*nomachi* marriages difficult. Secondly, most of the *nomachi* were very small in population. The rural town in Yoshimatsu district, for example, was depleted in population from an original eighteen households to eight households. According to the petitioners, "The men are all without wives, so that the town will be unable to survive, and gradually it will become difficult to perform the services for the daimyo" [ch. XV. 23]. Population depletion and the imbalanced sex ratio were given as reasons for seeking a modification of *han* marriage rules in thirteen of the fifty-six cases. The frequent mention of the shortage of women suggests that infanticide perhaps prevailed in impoverished villages. Poverty was cited in forty-one of the above cases.

The above indicates that the rural towns of Satsuma were not bustling centers of commerce. They existed primarily for the convenience of the government and their opportunities for development were greatly limited by innumerable restrictions placed upon travel and movement within the *han*. Even the increasing commercialization of agriculture resulting from the Tempō reforms could not materially benefit most of these rural towns because in Satsuma specialized crops were *han* monopolies.

On the other hand, internal evidence from the *Jōmoku* suggests that the situation for rural towns in Satsuma was improving. After the mid-eighteenth century the restrictions against *zaigō-nomachi* marriage alliances were increasingly set aside. Even so, for most *nomachi* the relaxation applied only to such marriages within the district or within immediately adjoining districts. Of the fifty-six *nomachi* which requested relief from marriage restrictions, twenty-five were permitted ties with other villagers within the district and

[5]Haraguchi Torao states there were 63 districts in Satsuma *han* having rural towns, and 52 districts with no rural towns. "Sappan machi kata no kenkyū" in Hidemura Senzō, ed., *Satsuma-han no Kiso Kōzō* (Tokyo, 1970), pp. 338–41.

twelve *nomachi* were allowed marriage relationship with one other district or with adjoining districts. Before 1800 the rural towns of Nojiri, Hazuki, and Kawanabe were exceptions in that they could choose mates from commoners located in four districts (including their own).

After 1799 the geographical range within which marriage ties for *nomachi* residents could be established was markedly improved. The chart below shows how the marriage network was extended for certain selected *nomachi*. The listing is in the order of appearance in the *Jōmoku*.

The two rural towns of Kokubu were especially favored by the *han*. Their residents were permitted marriages with commoners over a wide area of Satsuma. These two towns were rare exceptions

Chart Illustrating Increasing
Range of Marriage Network for Selected *Nomachi*

District Name of *nomachi*	Before 1799	1799–1820	1820–1838	1838–1852
Tsuruda	(1759) = 1		(1824) = 1 − ND	(1838) = 4
Ei		(1815) = 8		
Yamada		(1815) = 5		
Ichiki	(1767) = 1		(1838) = 9	
Hazuki	(1770) = 4	(1799) = 5	(1823) = 6	
Imaizumi	(1765) = 1 − ND		(1837) = 4	(1847) = 9
Ōmura	(1772) = 1 − ND		(1825) = 4	(1838) = 6
Kokubu*	(1786) = general			(1847) = 15+3**
Kawanabe	(1776) = 4	(1799) = 5		(1839) = 6
Hanaoka		(1805) = 1	(1825) = 5	
Chiran		(1800) = 6		
Hiwaki		(1815) = 4		
Kanoya				(1838) = 10+3**
Aira				(1848) = 10

Note: In parenthesis is the year in which relaxation of marriage restrictions was approved; number following is the number of districts with which the *nomachi* was permitted to establish marriage relationships. 1 = own district only; 1-ND own district + neighboring districts. *Kokubu had two *nomachi* which were given permission in 1786 to marry commoners generally throughout the *han*. **Figure includes the 3 *machi* in Kagoshima city.

in that neither pleaded poverty or depleting population as excuses for a relaxed marriage policy. There were several other towns whose matrimonial opportunities were greatly expanded. In such cases, though poverty is pleaded, one may well wonder whether such pleas had not simply become bureaucratic jargon. Any rural town requesting an extension of its marriage contacts would have to utilize this formula for official approval. Expansion of the marriage network over several districts indicates a wider range of contacts for the rural merchants. Wider contacts probably improved their business.

One other fact may be pointed out with reference to *nomachi* marriage relationships. Generally after 1800, petitions for marriages with people outside of the *nomachi* were granted for fixed periods of ten, fifteen, or twenty years. These permits were consistently renewed with only occasional short lapses between periods. Considering the fact that most *nomachi* petitioned for wider marriage contacts on the plea of poverty, it is interesting that several of the fixed periods were not renewed in later years. Six of the fixed periods were allowed to lapse in 1846, four in 1847, and one each in 1833, 1839, and 1844. Though from this tenuous evidence varying interpretations are possible, one may suggest that these lapses reflected improved economic conditions.

Like the *nomachi*, most *ura* and *hama* villages were small and poor. Though classified as fishing communities, these villagers had need to supplement their income through agriculture. Over thirty *ura, hama,* or *han-ura* villages located in eighteen districts are mentioned as having been granted special permission to marry commoners outside of their particular communities. In the great majority of cases fishing villagers were allowed marriages with other types of villagers, but only within their local district or including neighbor districts.

However, as in the case of the *nomachi*, the exceptions are of interest. In the district of Ei "several" fishing villages were granted permission to marry peasants and rural townspeople over an area of nine districts. Though poverty was pleaded, the range of marriage ties hints of rather extensive business contacts. For two fishing villages of Imaizumi (Takameura and Sezakiura) extra-village marital relationships were permitted in 1826 within the same district, but in 1847 the privilege was extended to include eight districts. Similarly, four fishing villages in Chiran were permitted such relationships within five districts in 1818 and six districts in 1848. Seven of the permits for relaxation of marriage rules, initially granted on the basis of poverty, ceased to be in effect between 1840 and 1850. It is, of course, difficult to state conclusively what the significance of this information is, but it points the direction which other scholarly inquiries might take.

3. Social Mobility for Commoners

As we have seen in the case of *gōshi,* it was possible for such low-ranking samurai and those whom we have described as quasi-samurai to be reduced to peasant status. Likewise, a person of common birth sometimes was permitted to wear a short sword and assume a surname. Such promotions of status were granted for a variety of reasons, such as the prestige of the leading family in the district, the significant functions assumed by local officials, or major financial contributions to the daimyo or philanthropic actions by individuals.

Both in the sections on the *nomachi* and on fishing villages, the *Jōmoku* provided for special privileges for the district of Kokubu. Kokubu had been a former castle-town of the Shimazu daimyo, Yoshihisa. Thus in various directives issued in 1785, 1801, 1824, 1830, and 1833 surnames were permitted for the village leader and sub-unit chiefs of the rural towns of Tōjinmachi and Komuramachi [ch. XV. 60–62] and the town and fishing village of Hamanoichi [ch. XVI. 40] and Hamamuraura [ch. XVI. 43] in Kokubu district. These privileges were granted "in special consideration of their background," "in consideration of their good lineage," or "by special consideration of the daimyo for its old history." Because Kokubu had been the territory of an illustrious forebear of the daimyo, officials previously without surnames suddenly acquired this symbol of status. The *myōzu,* the head of a village subunit (household collectives), was required to have a grant of land for his residence in order to qualify for the honor. It is not clear what political or other consideration motivated the *han* government to take such action in these particular years. "Good lineage" also was the reason for permitting the use of the Yotsumoto surname by a family in the fishing village of Matsuzakimachi in Taniyama district [ch. XVI. 12].

Often the *myōzu* in villages located near the *han* border were permitted surnames in order to give them more prestige when they encountered officials from other *han*. This was the case in the rural town of Takajō district, Morokata county [ch. XV. 65]. Since the townsmen assisted the local *ashigaru* and *gōshi* gendarmes in apprehending criminals, the *myōzu*'s duties sometimes required him to enter the neighboring *han*. A similar dispensation in the use of surnames was granted to the *myōzu* in the border fishing village in Shibushi district [ch. XVI. 31]. Here, in addition to the *myōzu*, the local village official (*machi-yaku*) also was permitted use of a surname during the period of his tenure.

Ship captains and regular boatmen who customarily wore swords were given added status in 1825 by the assumption of surnames on the authority of the *han* [ch. XVI. 2]. The reason for this was similar to the above, for the daimyo desired his men to have every advantage possible in their dealings with non-Satsuma people.

People and communities with special skills also were favored by the daimyo. Gold miners of Yamagano and Kago and tin miners of Taniyama were permitted surnames, and they entered into marriage relations with people of *gōshi* and *ashigaru* ranks or lower [ch. XVIII. 10–13]. Seventeen residents of Naishirogawa were permitted to retain their Korean family names, though the *Jōmoku* hedged by stating that these were clan names, not to be considered as surnames. Five of these Korean potters were singled out, however, and rewarded with *gōshi* status. One of these was Boku Taijun, who was rewarded for "several decades of service as Korean interpreter" [ch. XIII. 1, 5]. Another interesting example of status award was that given to Fujimoto Hikoroku and his successors. Fujimoto was the *myōzu* of the outcaste community. For his "especially meritorious service to the daimyo," he and his family for future generations were permitted not only the surname, but the imprint of the Fujimoto seal on the register in an upright position [ch. XXIV. 4]. Others of this community had their seals stamped sideways.

As can be seen by the foregoing there was some opportunity for local officials in the rural towns and fishing villages to be elevated in status. Even miners, potters, and influential members of the *eta* community were given surnames in recognition of their special services. However, no *myōzu* in any *zaigō* is mentioned in the *Jōmo-ku* as eligible to assume a surname. Perhaps this was due to the fact that there were thousands of *gōshi* (all with surnames) available in the agricultural districts. Any special task which a peasant might perform could be done by the *gōshi*. Apparently opportunities for amassing substantial wealth also were limited to a few rural merchants and residents of coastal villages.

Among rural townsmen, the *Jōmoku* cites the special case of two brothers in Takarabe district who distinguished themselves by assisting the poor and making frequent contributions of timber (cryptomeria trees) and money to help relieve the daimyo's debts. For their public spirit they were granted the right to use a surname and wear a short sword for the period of their lifetime (though one of the two brothers received the honor posthumously). Possibly because of the temporary nature of the grant, the surname is not mentioned in the document [ch. XV. 59]. The rural town in the district of Sueyoshi also received special recognition for reasons unstated. In 1786 twenty-eight of the residents were socially elevated by permission to use surnames, and in 1800 three other families were added to this list [ch. XV. 69, 78].

Shipping and trading activities for the coastal villages of Satsuma produced several outstanding entrepreneurs. From the *ura-machi* in Fukuyama district two brothers, Hyōuemon and Yahei, were posthumously recognized for their contributions to mitigate the disaster caused by the Sakurajima eruption of 1786. They (retroactively) and their heirs were granted the adoption of a surname and given "the same status as Kagoshima townsmen" [ch. XVI. 23]. The latter reference indicates that many townsmen were privileged merchants with surnames, often with the status of *hitokerai,* a special retainer rank for merchants. Suda Gihei of the *uramachi* of Uchinoura district also was honored for his generosity in relief work. His surname was allowed posthumously but the privilege was extended to his successors [ch. XVI. 24]. Similar honors were given to Koreeda Sukeemon (posthumously) and Koreeda Sukejūrō, residents of the coastal village of Matsuzaki-machi in Taniyama district, the same village as that of Yotsumoto, earlier mentioned as a recipient of a surname because of his "good lineage." The Koreedas had twice contributed funds to the dai-myo's coffer. Initially their surname was allowed for one gener-ation, but later it was made a hereditary right [ch. XVI. 35].

Among the most notable of these capitalistic benefactors were Hamazaki Taheiji of Minatoura and Yoshizaki Yauemon of Suri-nohama. Both were granted hereditary rights to a surname be-cause of their special services to the daimyo [ch. XVI. 28]. Minatoura and Surinohama were located in Ibusuki district, an area economically significant because its ports were well-protected from seasonal typhoons. Ibusuki also was endowed with salubrious hot springs, providing the basis for its major tourist industry today, and from the terse entry in the *Jōmoku,* we may surmise that Hamazaki and Yoshizaki were munificent hosts who entertained the great daimyo, Shimazu Shigehide, as he relaxed at his favorite spa. Here was an opportunity for commoners to establish an inti-mate relationship with their *han* lord.

Household relationships

In Satsuma, as in other parts of Japan, individuals were not independent autonomous beings; they were officially regarded in terms of their membership in a household. Everyone except members of the most prestigious families were required to carry household tags. Members of the household were family members, retainers, servants, and employees [e.g., see ch. XVIII. 3]. More-over, in each household someone had to assume responsibility for its membership, so that if a household head was charged with a crime and removed from this responsibility the remaining members of his family usually were assigned to the household of a relative [ch. XVII. 2–5, 8; ch. XX. 1, 8, 10].

The terms *kerai* and *kachū* give etymological emphasis to the household. Both of these terms refer to retainers, but we have chosen to translate the former as "attendant(s)" and the latter as "retainer(s)" for convenience. *Kerai* was a general term for a retainer or attendant. All castle-town samurai and *gōshi* were the daimyo's *kerai*, but many of these samurai had *kerai* of their own. The term was applicable to both samurai and commoner attendants. The term *kachū*, however, referred to samurai who served the vassals of the *han* lord. Thus the *kachū* was the retainer of his immediate master and a subretainer in terms of the *han* lord. According to the regulations, a castle-town *kerai* who transferred his services to become a *kachū* could not return to his former status [ch. XVIII. 27].

Samurai retainers [*kachū*] generally identified themselves in the registration process in terms of the household of their master. However, the retainers of the eight Shimazu families of *dokurei* status entered the name of the private territory to which they belonged instead of the name of their liege lord [ch. II. 11, 14, 24]. This, of course, indicated that the retainers belonged to a powerful vassal with land holdings equal to that of a minor daimyo. Retainers of other *dokurei* status officials (the highest officers in the *han*) registered the fact that they were the retainers "of the household of Lord so-and-so," [ch. III. 5] while retainers of officials of *chakuza* status [from *yoriai-nami* rank to *isshomochi* rank] recorded their membership with "the household of so-and-so," the honorific title "lord" being omitted [ch. III. 5]. Retainers of officials of less than *yoriai* rank were also identified as being "of the household of so-and-so." But at the lower end of the scale, if the official was only a one-generation *koban*, his attendants listed themselves as "retainer of so-and-so," the term "household" being omitted [ch. IV. 1]. Such distinctions officially established the prestige of the household, which in turn reflected on the social importance of all its members.

The prestige of the family was influenced by, but was not coincident with, the status of the household. The household was a legal corporate entity with certain rights and prerogatives assigned thereto. If a member of the family, let us say a younger son, decided to leave the household or establish a branch family and was given permission to do so, he thereby lost the prerogatives of membership in the main household. Conversely, when a member of a family gained status by admittance to membership in a larger household, his new privileges did not necessarily extend equally to all members of his family [ch. VIII. 22–24]. Eligibility for membership into the household thus was a matter for state regulation, not a right accrued from blood relationship.

Depending on the status of the household the terms defining relationships, such as wife, daughter, and male and female servants, differed. Wives of the highest-ranking families were registered as *"oku* of so-and-so" [ch. II. 7], those of *chakuza* status were recorded as *"uchi* of so-and-so" [ch. III. 1], and wives of lower-ranking samurai were simply listed as *"tsuma"* [ch. IV. 3]. Daughters of samurai were recognized as *"joshi,"* but daughters of commoners were registered as *"musume"* [ch. IV. 6]. Female attendants of households of the rank of *koban* and above were recorded as *"naijo"* [ch. II. 14; ch. IV. 1], while for lesser status they were listed as *"tsukai-onna"* or *"gejo"* [ch. IV. 2; ch. XI. 5]. Male servants of a *koban* rank household were *"kerai,"* but if the household heir was a minor, his servants were denigrated to *genin* status [ch. II. 1; ch. XI. 6, 7]. Mistresses and concubines were given official recognition as "true mother" when they gave birth to the household master's "true son" or "true child." However, the status of such "true mother" was inferior to that of the legal spouse [ch. II. 5; ch. IV. 4]. Adopted and foster children were specifically identified as such in the register [ch. VII. 8. See also ch. XXIII. 3]. Since these status terms were relative to the status of other people in Satsuma society, they were especially important for the individual in terms of his or her field for marriage relationships.

In this connection, it is interesting that a special chapter in the *Jōmoku* is concerned solely with regulations concerning the ladies serving in the daimyo's residence [ch. VII]. It may be noted first that such ladies were recruited from even the most common ranks, probably chosen for their personal charm [ch. XIII. 2]. Provision is made even for daughters from Naishirogawa, the Korean community of potters, who serve as *otsugi*. Secondly, although maids designated as *ohanshita,* the lowest rank of the daimyo's female attendants, were not eligible for marriage with samurai, those of *otsugi* rank or higher, "though they be from families of *hitokerai* (commoners serving as purveyors and licensed as retainers), townsmen, fishermen, peasants, or temple-gate personnel, shall be permitted to marry samurai," provided their services had been fully satisfactory [ch. VII. 2]. These ladies were given samurai status by having them adopted by a *gōshi* or samurai family. Moreover, stated the regulation, "If by chance a person finds it difficult . . . [to request inclusion into a samurai or *gōshi*] family, instructions will be issued by the steward of the grand chamber . . ." [ch. VII. 4]. Rendering personal services to the daimyo clearly was a channel for upward social mobility even for those of humble origin.

There were constant pressures for upward mobility, but these were countered by regulative restrictions. We have seen above that a *koban* samurai could not adopt a *gōshi* without a demotion for himself. Among the more interesting regulations which limited mobility within the family were those governing the ranking of boys. Ranking by age was a natural system, of course; normally the oldest son succeeded his father as head of the family. However, in case the natural son was not a fit candidate because of physical or mental debilities, or if there were no suitable males to succeed the family head, it was permissible to adopt sons from outside of the family [ch. X. 2]. When there were several natural sons, the departure of the eldest from the family enabled remaining sons to move up, the second son becoming number one, the third son becoming number two, etc. This was called "*otoko agari,*" or "moving up of sons." In the case of families of good lineage of *koban* rank and higher, these rankings of sons had special significance, for gifts were presented to the daimyo in proportion to their particular position in the family. The moving up of sons, therefore, required official regulations.

According to these regulations, if the natural heir died or was adopted by another family, a petition was required to move up the number two son to the position of heir. However, the moving up of the number three and younger sons was not permitted unless the petitioning family was privileged to present gifts to the daimyo.

This gift-giving relationship with the daimyo was important, for if the eldest son of a family which did not have this privilege was adopted by another family only to return later to his original family, he was restored to his position of heir. In a similar situation in the case of a privileged family, if the former heir returned from his adoptive family, he was relegated to the last place of his natural family. Moreover, if the eldest son in a family which did not have gift-giving privileges established a branch family, he was given the number two position of his natural family, but in the case of the higher status family, the same son under similar circumstances became last in the ranking of his natural family. These restrictions, however, did not preclude petitions for designating the number three or younger son as heir should the position be otherwise vacant [ch. VIII. 6, 7].

For the samurai class the offsprings of mistresses and concubines only required verification of the status of "true child" or "true mother," but for commoners the laws were more complex. Peasants, rural townsmen, fishermen, and temple-gate personnel who were granted specific permission to marry outside of their community were required to obtain "wife" tags for their spouses [ch. XV. 15; ch. XVI. 4]. If such tags had not been requested, the marriage was illegal and both parties were heavily fined. The government assumed in such cases that the female had been sent to the household, not as a wife, but as an employee, and thus children resulting from such a relationship belonged to the employer if he was a resident of a rural community.

Because the government regarded rural communities as corporate productive units, the tendency was to give priority to the economic functions of the community rather than to the rights of the individual child and its natural mother. Such a functional view inclined the regulations to regard common people as property, and this in turn created relationships in the household which bordered on slavery. It was stated, for example, that "Those who have been sold to peasants by samurai, *gōshi,* or anyone else, and who have certificates of the agricultural magistrate, even though they have not yet received [new] tags, shall be prohibited from returning to their former employers" [ch. XV. 3]. Moreover, if a commoner woman gave birth to children during the period of her term employment, these children belonged to her employer regardless of who fathered them [ch. XI. 11]. Of course, the term employment of the woman required official approval. If she had been illegally employed, particularly on a non-term basis, the employer was not entitled to her children [ch. XXII. 9].

A form of illegal household servitude, which may have been prevalent, judging from the numerous injunctions and heavy fines assigned, was to take in a woman nominally as a bride, but in fact using her in lieu of interest payment on a debt owed by her family. If such a woman did not have a "wife" tag in the household of her alleged employment, the government assumed she was so employed, and did not allow for any excuses by the parties concerned [chs. XII. 16; XV. 1, 10, 15; XXII. 9; also a related situation in ch. XXII. 16]. When there was an offspring from such illegal relationships the government considered the advantages to itself in assigning the child to its place of registration. The interests of the child or its parents were secondary.

The detailed instructions for verification of each child, whether it be a natural child, adoptive child, or foster child, were based on the assumption that the household and family were more than natural social institutions. They were legal institutions subject to the controls of the *han*. While verification procedures differed with ranks and status, generally two witnesses were required from the *kumi* in the case of the samurai [ch. VIII. 4, 10–12] and two witnesses from the neighborhood unit in the case of commoners. In addition, supporting statements of officials were necessary before entry in the register became legal.

Procedures for checking movements of people

To establish a complete social control policy it was not enough to define the social position and functional role of each person. An elaborate checking system was required. Status and function and other details were entered into the household register as well as on individual identification tags, and these were periodically investigated and checked. Though tags were small much information could be transmitted to the inspector by brief "side notations" alongside the name identifying the bearer with greater or lesser lords, institutions, or households, by the entry or non-entry of surname and/or age, by the classificatory names of villages of residence, by the upper or lower, upright or sideways, placing of seals, etc.

As we have seen, checking stations were established at border entry points, at mountain passes, and at various places, along highways and less-travelled byways. Anyone entering or departing a district in Satsuma was required to report to the proper authorities and their tags checked or exchanged. This applied to people who were leaving or entering for purposes of marriage, adoption, or divorce, short-term or long-term employment, business and official trips, and pilgrimages. Regulations also established procedures for checking criminals, exiles, those placed under custody, runaways, wandering mendicants, and other "floating persons" (ukiyonin).

People entering the han, whether outsiders or Satsuma persons returning home, were all issued new tags. People departing from Satsuma left their tags behind, though an exception seems to have been made for seamen voyaging to the Ryukyu Kingdom, a dependency of Satsuma. [Seamen who lost their tags due to a shipwreck on such a trip were exonerated upon reporting the circumstances. ch. XXII. 3]. Outside priests and skilled workers coming into the han were assigned to a responsible religious institution or employer, which fact was noted on the tag along with their previous affiliation, place of origin, and whether their stay in Satsuma was temporary or permanent. Departure and entry procedures were similar for Satsuma exiles or for offenders against the Bakufu who were sent to Satsuma for custody [ch. XIX. 1–3; ch. XX. 3–6].

The control system for movement of people within the han required the coordination of local officials at the village of departure and village of entry. Procedures for tag and register adjustments depended upon whether the change of residence by the individual was short term or permanent. When such movements took place these names were placed in special departure or entry registers which were periodically exchanged between officials to check for discrepancies [ch. XXI. 6].

Every effort was made to place individuals in households or religious institutions which assumed responsibility for their conduct. Occasionally petitions were granted to remove oneself from the household register in order to become an *angya* (a wandering mendicant) [ch. XXIV. 2]. Religious mendicants, wandering (mountain) priests, minstrels, soothsayers, etc. were regarded with some suspicion by the authorities, but perhaps more troublesome were a small number of the "floating persons" who failed to record to which jurisdiction they belonged. The regulation called for special care in investigating such cases. When they were discovered the procedure was to assign them to a peasant village [ch. XXIII. 7]. In this category was an outcaste group of beggars, *hinin* ("non-humans"), who did not carry tags. Since their style of life did not conform to the hard-working pattern of peasants, the official instructions provided that "Although according to law those who are not under any specific supervision shall be assigned to become peasants, if it is determined upon investigation that a beggar, who was ordered to become a peasant, has been useless, he shall receive his tag from the *eta* community of his district. . . ." [ch. XXIV. 3]. No doubt the government did not wish such beggars to be liabilities to peasant communities rather than adding to their productive labor force.

Finally, various provisions were designed to discourage sins of deliberate or inadvertent commission or omission which made investigative and control procedures more difficult. Secret harboring of outsiders and runaways was a crime which, of course, made the offender liable to arrest [ch. XXIII. 9]. Samurai and *gōshi* escapees from the *han* who were returned suffered various disabilities such as loss of samurai status and surname, placement in custody of a relative, prohibition of adoption of an heir or of establishing branch households, and exclusion from official service. On his tag were recorded the circumstances of his escape and return and the notation, "Returned runaway; forbidden to depart for other domain" [ch. XVII. 5–7].

Heavy penalties were imposed for damaging, effacing, or losing identification tags. It did not matter whether such effacement was due to the innocent act of a child or the appetite of wood-worms, or that the loss was incurred by theft. If a person presented proof that he had lost his tag he was fined two-hundred *mon* copper, but five hundred *mon* if he had no proof. Proof of loss by fire also was required. False entries, such as "true child," "foster child," or "adopted child" were causes for particularly heavy fines, which were measured out to the parents, would-be parents, and varying levels of responsible officials [ch. XXII].

4. Summary and Conclusion

An analysis of the *Shūmon tefuda aratame jōmoku* does not turn up evidence of a seriously deteriorating society in Satsuma. On the contrary, the regulations suggest that the government was quite aware of certain population imbalances and was capable of making necessary adjustments to long-standing regulations. The regulations tightened the traditional system, perhaps making it even more responsive to political authority than had been the case in the past.

In the very process of defining the relative social standing of the upper class in Satsuma, individuals were made aware of their personal relationship to the daimyo and their dependence on him for continued enjoyment of their privileges. Moreover, once their status was defined in explicit terms it would have been difficult for any ambitious person to alter his standing without special approval from the *han* lord. The well-defined status system, therefore, provided stability among the most influential people.

Within the relatively static status system it was possible for men of special ability to be given positions above their social station. Such responsibilities were awarded by one-generation appointments to a higher status rank. One could also display merit and gain social recognition by climbing the social ladder in the religious hierarchy by dint of hard study and successful negotiation of examinations.

Most important of all, however, was the enormous power and authority of the daimyo. It was his prerogative to award social prestige even to commoners who served him well. The daimyo was above the *han* regulations, which were devised by his own officials.

There are no regulations in the *Jōmoku* which placed any restrictions whatsoever on the authority of the *han* lord. While he had need to establish order among his vassals and retainers, he could bypass the bureaucratic establishment in selecting his own personal attendants and assistants. It was this channel of personal service to the daimyo that was utilized by Lord Shimazu Shigehide in elevating Zusho Shōzaemon from tea server to *karō* in order that the latter could institute the Tempō Reforms. It was this same channel which Lord Shimazu Nariakira utilized to appoint Saigō Takamori as his yardman and thence to a position of greatest trust within the *han* during the critical Bakumatsu period. By the same token the great importance of the daimyo invited fierce political struggles over questions of succession. The earlier half of the nineteenth century indeed was marked by bloody purges accompanying each transfer of power. Once the transfer was accomplished, discipline was tight, and possibilities for the rebelliously inclined were remote. The details of the *Jōmoku* provide us insights as to the degree of control the *han* exercised over the lives of the people.

Moreover, although as seen by contemporary eyes the controls would seem intolerable, the chances for organized resistance by the common people of Satsuma in mid-nineteenth century were remote. The sophisticated surveillance and investigation system with elaborate checks by different authorities, the great number of officials present at every local community, the restrictions and controls on travel, and the relative isolation of rural communities account for the fact that Satsuma was unique among the domains of Japan in the virtual absence of peasant uprisings. To be sure there were problems of runaways, i.e., people seeking relief from oppression by escaping to other regions, and there were occasional disturbances involving faithful members of the Ikkō sect. The latter incidents have sometimes been described as a form of peasant uprisings, but it is probable that this sect continued to thrive despite official repressive policy because the believers of this faith were not limited to peasants, but included many in the samurai class. In this sense the Ikkō sect transcended class lines, and perhaps constituted a threat to the social order.

The rigidity of functional differentiation of rural villages was also being moderated by the beginning of the nineteenth century.

This is evident in the extension of the marriage network between different types of villages and on an inter-district scale. This extension of marital relationships also suggests a widening trade pattern for at least a few of the rural towns and fishing villages. Certainly in the latter communities some individuals had acquired sufficient wealth to gain the favor of the *han* lord. Increasingly toward the middle of the nineteenth century the services of rural townsmen and of fishing villagers were required to service official travel. In the same period the Tempō Reforms designed to establish and tighten *han* monopolies as well as to increase production and make distribution more efficient undoubtedly stimulated general economic activity within the *han*.

The existence of specialized communities in Satsuma, such as Naishirogawa and the gold and tin mining communities, illustrates the interest of the Satsuma government in certain monopoly products. Naishirogawa was (and still is today) a community of Koreans who perpetuated a generations-old tradition of producing pottery with distinctive deep-black glaze. To encourage production of this Satsuma product the regulations provided for in-marriages of women and restricted the outflow of the population. Special concessions and favors were granted, such as allowing the Korean families to retain their "clan names," honoring their leading members with *gōshi* status, and occasionally selecting their beauties for employment in the daimyo's residence. Additionally, the case of Boku Taijun, who was rewarded with *gōshi* status for his services as interpreter, is evidence that Korean-Satsuma contacts were not insignificant.

Similarly, gold and tin mining were activities controlled and fostered by the *han*. For these enterprises people with technical skills were imported into the *han* and placed under the jurisdiction of a special official, the magistrate of gold mines. Not only were they permitted surnames and allowed to marry daughters of *ashigaru* and *gōshi* status, their area for establishing marriage relationships was exceptionally wide: eight districts for the miners of the Yamagano gold mine [ch. XVIII. 11], six districts for workers of the Kago gold mine [ch. XVIII. 12], and five districts for the residents at the Taniyama tin mine [ch. XVIII. 13]. Although gold mining was presumed to be a Bakufu monopoly, it is interesting that Bakufu authority is nowhere reflected in this connection in the *Jōmoku*.

In all of the above, one is initially struck by the extreme conservatism and traditionalism which seemed to prevail in Satsuma. On closer examination, however, one might suggest that rather than its commitment to traditionalism a more important characteristic of Satsuma was its pragmatic orientation. So long as the traditions served their purpose, they were maintained, but when the *han* interests dictated a change, the rules and regulations were modified without apologies. Benefit to the daimyo was sufficient reason for change. It will be noted that the *Jōmoku* is singularly devoid of moralistic or ideological rationalization. On the date that this *Jōmoku* was issued in 1852 Japan could not have been aware of the basic changes in the political order which were to take place in the ensuing two decades, but the Satsuma leadership was capable of retaining control over its regimented social base while shifting its political policies as circumstances dictated.

Part 2
TRANSLATION OF
THE *SHŪMON TEFUDA ARATAME JŌMOKU*

I. Regulations on the investigation of religious sects and identification tags

In compliance with the Bakufu proscription of Christianity, religious sect identification tags were issued long ago for the entire population of the lord's domain. Accordingly, the following pertain to regulations concerning Christianity and the Ikkō sect in connection with the present directive for tag inspections.

1. Special care shall be taken in investigating Christian sects. Persons about whom there is any doubt should be arrested immediately and reported. Moreover, the Ikkō sect, which is prohibited within the lord's domain, also shall be carefully investigated. Of course, persons who are affiliated with this sect shall be reported.

2. Concerning the Ikkō sect, since the investigation of the third year of Hōei (1706), if a person is found to be a leader [of the sect] in possession of Buddhist images, scriptures, and other Buddhist furnishings, he and members of his household of both sexes, fifteen years of age and over, are given written instructions from the office of sect investigation concerning the entry of a side notation on their tags. The side notation, "formerly Ikkō sect," shall be entered on their tags and in the register. But even a present member of the above household shall not be required to make a side notation if he joined the household after the Buddhist images, etc., had been turned over [to the authorities]. Of course, a person of the above household who is required to write "formerly Ikkō sect" in a side

45

notation shall continue to do so even though he is now a member of a different household. Again, when a person who should have a side notation recorded goes to another area, the investigative officials of the two areas shall check with each other and record "formerly Ikkō sect" on his tag and in the register. When both investigative officials have returned to Kagoshima, the situation shall be reported to the office of religious sect inspection.

Proviso: When an adherent of the said sect is given a written memorandum in the above manner, the side notation is required for the head of the household alone. His wife and children are excused from side notations, but because they may be inclined toward the Ikkō sect, a detailed investigation shall be made. If there is any doubt about anyone, he shall be reported promptly to the office of religious sect inspection.

3. If the side notation, "formerly Ikkō sect," was entered on a person's tag at the time of the previous inspection, the same shall be entered on his new tag.

4. Written instructions have been issued by the office of religious sect inspection concerning individuals who had been reduced to peasant status for the crime of belonging to the Ikkō sect and then restored to their former status because they informed on others; and individuals who had been discovered earlier to be of the Ikkō sect and ordered to have a side notation entered, who then belatedly turned in their Buddhist images, scriptures, and other religious furnishings. These people shall be issued tags like their former ones. The side notation, "formerly Ikkō sect," shall be omitted only from their tags, and important information shall be noted and entered in detail in the register.

5. There are persons who, having harbored Buddhist images, scriptures, and furnishings of the Ikkō sect in past years, turned them in during the recent Ikkō sect inspection, alleging that these had been kept by relatives, servants, or *nago,* and denying that they themselves were members of the sect. There has been an order since the fifth year of Empō (1677) that such persons shall be reported, but even now they exist. Careful inquiries shall be made of suspicious persons, and if they are found to be members of the Ikkō sect, they shall be reported immediately to the office of religious sects.

6. Buddhist priests, mountain priests, sorceresses, itinerant blind lutists, imprecators, astrologers, and other soothsayers, when they pray, secretly assert and deceive their listeners that their's is the Buddha statuary which has been worshipped since the olden days of their ancestors, or that the image was that revered as the Amida of the Ikkō sect. As a consequence followers of the Ikkō sect have not been stamped out. Henceforth whenever there are such people, not only they, but all others in their group shall be punished. This order shall be transmitted to all officials of the district without fail.

7. All those who must enter a side notation, "formerly Ikkō sect," on their tags and in the register, and those who are excused from such a notation on their tags but who must enter such a notation in the register, shall have their tags checked against the inspection register, and their names shall be entered in a separate volume. When such people die, their names shall be removed from the master register of the office of religious sect investigation, and this fact shall be recorded at the back of the above-mentioned separate volume which shall be turned over to the office of religious sect inspection.

II. Regulations on the inspection of *go-ichimon* and of Shimazu Shimofusa, Shimazu Wakasa, Shimazu Tosho, Shimazu Buzen, and of those who are granted the privilege of individual audience, and of those whose standing is equivalent to or higher than the standing of the grand overseer, and of those whose stipends are more than ten thousand *koku*

1. Concerning the following eight persons, Lord Shimazu Suhō, Lord Shimazu Hyōgo, Lord Shimazu Sanuki, Lord Shimazu Aki, Shimazu Shimofusa, Shimazu Wakasa, Shimazu Tosho, and Shimazu Buzen, they and their wives and the husbands and wives of their succeeding two generations shall be exempt from bearing tags. The retired heads of these families and their widows also shall be so exempt.

2. Sons of the daimyo who are adopted as heirs into families which do not have the privilege of individual audience shall be exempt, along with their wives, from bearing a tag, and their adoptive parents also shall be so exempt.

Proviso: Even if a person does not have the privilege of individual audience, if his wife is the daughter of the daimyo, both he and his wife are exempt from bearing tags as long as they are married. The tag exemption applies even after he is retired or after she becomes a widow.

3. When a son of the daimyo enters by adoption into a family which does not have the privilege of individual audience, and his true mother accompanies him, she is exempt from the need for a "true mother" tag.

Proviso: When a daughter of the daimyo marries into a similar situation the above provision shall apply.

4. When a person's office gives him the privilege of an individu-

48

al audience, he and his parents are exempt from carrying tags.

5. When a person with the privilege of individual audience either by family status or by office is the child of a concubine, his natural mother must obtain a tag.

6. All younger sons and all daughters of Lord Shimazu Suhō, Lord Shimazu Hyōgo, Lord Shimazu Sanuki, and Lord Shimazu Aki shall be exempt from wearing tags for so long as they stay within the family.

Proviso: If they establish branch families, are adopted, or get married, they shall be governed according to the status of their new families.

7. The keeper of the castle, senior councilors, liaison officials of the daimyo, junior elders, the grand overseer, and the grand overseer equivalent, along with their wives, are exempt from tags for so long as they are in office. After they are excused from office they must obtain tags. Wives of those of *go-ichimon* rank, of those who have the privilege of individual audience, of the keeper of the castle, and of the senior councilors shall record in the register of tag inspection " '*oku*' of so-and-so."

8. Those whose stipends are 10,000 *koku* or more, their wives, the husbands and wives of the second and third generations in direct line of succession, and including those who retire or become widows, are all exempt from carrying tags.

9. For those whose status or office is that of *go-ichimon,* senior councilor, *isshomochi, isshomochi-kaku, yoriai, yoriai-kaku* [*sic, yoriai-nami*], personal steward of the lord, public steward, town magistrate, personal attendant of the lord, or the lord's personal attendant-equivalent, it is sufficient that their [subordinate] officials stamp the seal on the various documents to be entered into the register of religious sect tag inspection. For all others the seals must be stamped personally.

10. When a child is born to any of the above personages, the testimonial seal of neighboring samurai is not required, and (the birth) shall be recorded in the register of religious tag inspection with the seal of their officials. Moreover, those who are exempt from tags shall be governed by their status.

Proviso: In cases of additions or departures of family members by adoption of sons or marriage of daughters in reciprocal relationships, the register shall be thoroughly checked with verifying statements of officials.

11. Samurai retainers in the service of Lord Shimazu Suhō, Lord Shimazu Sanuki, Lord Shimazu Aki, Shimazu Shimofusa, Shimazu Wakasa, Shimazu Tosho, and Shimazu Buzen shall not record their ages, but they shall record their names on the tags. Side notations of the names of their liege lords are not required, but the name of the district which constitutes the private domain of each of the households shall be recorded. Female servants shall be recorded as *"naijo,"* but their ages shall be omitted from the tags. In the register both samurai retainers and *naijo* shall record their ages.

12. The family head and wife, and their successors for one generation of the following twelve families, Beppu, Nakamura, Higo, Niiro, Soki, Hino, Machida, Kawakami, Machida, Kondō, Kurikawa, and Yano, being attendants of Lord Shimazu Suhō, Lord Shimazu Hyōgo, Lord Shimazu Sanuki, and Lord Shimazu Aki, are exempt from recording their ages on their tags and in the register. When daughters of these attendants marry, as in the case of castle-town samurai, they are excused from recording their social status.

13. The following twelve families, Umemoto Shichiemon, Ogata Kizaemon, Nakamura Sanjūrō, Kawakami Kyūemon, Hishijima Kyūzaemon, Honda Kogengo, Ijūin Hachibei, Yasuyama Sanzaemon, Umemoto Heizaemon, Kabayama Sukezaemon, Takuma Hikosuke, and Urakawa Mokuuemon, being attendants of the above four (liege) families, upon their petition of the third year of Enkyō (1746), were granted a status immediately below that of the twelve families mentioned in the preceding article. Consequently in all matters concerning their tags, register, and marriages, the regulations of the above article shall apply.

14. Samurai retainers of Lord Shimazu Hyōgo are exempt from recording their ages on their tags and in the register. Side notation of the name of their lord is not required, but they must record the name of the district which constitutes the lord's domain. The [lord's] female servants shall be recorded as *"naijo."* Moreover, when daughters of samurai retainers and persons carrying *naijo* tags marry castle-town samurai, *yoriki* attached to various

[functional] groups, or *gōshi*, they are exempt from recording their ages on their tags and in the register, but their social status shall be recorded. This was so ordered, on the basis of a petition, in the second year of An'ei (1773).

15. When the progenitor of the line of Lord Shimazu Hyōgo was granted the domain of Kajiki, more than 370 castle-town warriors were ordered to remain there [as his attendants]. Among their descendants some were recalled to the castle-town and some families have ceased to exist for various reasons. The heads of the presently remaining 317 families and their heirs for the next two generations henceforth shall indicate that they are "so-and-so, of (one of the 317 families)." Members of branch families of the above, as in the past, shall not record their ages either on their tags or in the register. Other attendants also, as in the past, shall not make side notations on their tags, but they shall note their ages in the register. This was so ordered on the second month, third year of Bunsei (1820).

16. Daughters of samurai retainers and those carrying *naijo* tags who are in the service of Lord Shimazu Suhō, Lord Shimazu Sanuki, Lord Shimazu Aki, Shimazu Shimofusa, Shimazu Wakasa, Shimazu Tosho, and Shimazu Buzen, upon marrying castle-town samurai, *yoriki* attached to various [functional] groups, or *gōshi*, shall record their ages only in the register, and on their tags they shall omit their ages and record only their social status.

17. One hundred thirteen attendants of Shimazu Buzen were ordered to serve as guards at the by-road of Kajiyama. Because they were remotely located in the mountains, they were unable to bring in by marriage daughters from among their peers. Thus, although contrary to regulations, upon their petition, thrice since the fifth year of Meiwa (1768) they were granted twenty-year periods during which they were allowed to marry daughters of shrine personnel, temple-gate personnel, rural townsmen, fishermen, and peasants. As these periods expired, again upon their petition, they were granted another twenty-year period as in the past, beginning with the first year of Kaei (1848).

18. Shimazu Buzen was given charge of the Kajiyama barrier, but the large amount of work for *ashigaru* in an area which borders another state has caused a problem of manpower. Therefore, wish-

ing to utilize rural townsmen of Miyakonojō in place of *ashigaru*, a petition was submitted to allow the rural townsmen to have surnames the same as for townsmen in border districts. Permission was granted to allow surnames only for *myōzu*.

19. Daughters of *ashigaru* and lackeys attached to offices, who are in the service of *ichimon* and *isshomochi*, are strictly forbidden from marrying castle-town warriors, *gōshi*, and *yoriki*, as ordered in the seventh month, seventh year of Bunsei (1824).

20. On the matter of writing surnames on the [upper right] side [of personal names], heretofore there has been no uniform style, since nothing had been prescribed by the Bakufu, of course, nor even by the *han* government. Henceforth, those who, instead of writing in a single column, have been writing [their names] on the side, as well as other people in the future, shall all write downwards [i.e., in a single column]. Moreover, inasmuch as there is a distinction as to who may marry samurai, it is ordered that past regulations governing status shall be followed. In addition, in the matter of writing [one's name] downwards, it is ordered that anyone who erroneously assumes that thereby his social status has changed, shall be deprived of his surname.

21. In Hishida village in Ōsaki district there is an area of *kakechi* of Miyakonojō on which thirty-five samurai retainers of Shimazu Buzen reside. Since they have been mistaken to be as of the same status as fishermen, by their request they are ordered to record on their tags, "Hishida Group, Miyakonojō."

22. Because there were very few *ashigaru* families in the service of Lord Shimazu Suhō, marriages with people of equal social status were difficult to arrange. Upon their request, for a period of ten years from the twelfth year of Tempō (1841), they were granted permission to take in by marriage the peasants of the various villages of Shigetomi and the villages under their liege lord's control in the district of Kamō, Tōgō, Kiyomizu, and Shibushi. This period expired in the third year of Kaei (1850).

23. Because there were very few families of *ashigaru* status belonging to Shimazu Wakasa marriages between people of equal social status were difficult to arrange. Thus, upon request, for a period of ten years from the twelfth year of Tempō (1841), they were granted permission to take in by marriage people from fishing

villages, rural towns, and various peasant villages of Hanaoka district. The period having expired, authorization was granted as in the past for another ten years beginning with the fourth year of Kaei (1851).

24. Lord Tanegashima Danjō by special consideration was granted for one generation a rank next to that of *ichimon* and at the top of the rank held by Shimazu Wakasa and his peers. Consequently, it was ordered in the sixth month, second year of Kōka (1845) that for the generation of Lord Danjō the regulations concerning the tags of his attendants shall be the same as for [attendants of] those bearing the Shimazu surname.

III. Regulations on the inspection of the ranks from *isshomochi* to *yoriai-nami*

1. Wives of those in the ranks of *isshomochi, isshomochi-kaku, yoriai,* and *yoriai-nami* shall record on their tags and in the register, " *'uchi'* of so-and-so."

2. When a person of *yoriai-nami* rank or higher acquires an heir by his concubine and he requests a "true mother" tag for this concubine, he shall make the request at the time of tag inspection. If his request is granted the *goyōnin* shall prepare a confirming statement. Upon verification of this statement a "true mother" tag shall be issued. Moreover, her age shall be omitted from her tag and from the register.

3. When a "true mother" tag is requested by those of *koban* rank or lower the above provision shall also apply. For those whose request is granted, a confirming statement shall be prepared by the magistrate of accounting. Upon verification of this statement, a "true mother" tag shall be issued. Moreover, both on the tag and in the register the [concubine's] age and social status shall be recorded.

4. Persons of *yoriai-nami* rank or higher, who from the past have requested "true mother" tags for their concubines who have been recording their ages [on their tags], and persons of *koban* rank or lower, whose concubines have been omitting their ages on their tags but have been receiving "true mother" tags, shall be allowed these past procedures, and new tags shall be issued accordingly.

54

5. Samurai retainers of *isshomochi, isshomochi-kaku, yoriai,* and *yoriai-nami* shall indicate their ages and surnames and the words, "of the household of so-and-so," both on the tags and in the register. Maid servants shall be indicated as *naijo* and their ages shall be recorded. Although some have followed this form for a long time, others have written their master's name on the margin of their tags, and in some cases their master's name was not recorded in the register. Henceforth the records must be uniform in style.

Proviso: Among the above, retainers of the keeper of the castle, of the senior councilors, and of those who are granted the privilege of individual audience with the daimyo, shall write "of the household of Lord so-and-so" as a side notation on their tags and in the register, thus following past regulations in adding the character "lord" to the name of their master.

6. Because there were few *ashigaru* families serving Shimazu Kaname, it was difficult to arrange marriages between social equals. Thus, upon request, permission was granted in the second year of Kōka (1845) for a period of ten years following, to bring in by marriage daughters of fishermen and peasants of Shinjō district.

IV. Matters concerning functional status and miscellaneous titles

1. As for those who are not of *yoriai-nami* rank or higher, but who serve as commander of the outer guards, magistrate of temples and shrines, magistrate of accounting, captain of an *okoshōgumi* guard unit, or chief duty officer, their attendants shall record their ages, surnames, and "of the household of so-and-so" on their tags and in the register. Female servants also shall write in "*naijo*" and record their ages. Even after their masters are relieved from their posts, since [the latter] have clearly fulfilled their duties, the attendants shall record their surnames as indicated above.

Proviso: Since these people serve the daimyo in the above functions for one generation, their descendants shall be treated in accordance with the previous status of their household.

2. As for those whose status is that of one-generation *koban* but who serve as magistrate of guns or in higher office, or even if they are not given any function but are assigned to the office of *jitō*, their attendants shall record their ages, surnames, and "attendant of so-and-so" on their tags. Female servants shall list themselves as "*tsukai-onna*" and shall record their ages. After their masters are relieved of their duties or from the office of *jitō*, the attendants shall make entries on their tags in accordance with the original status of the household.

3. Various officials, both castle-town samurai and lesser status, shall have their wives recorded as "*tsuma*."

4. A castle-town samurai whose marriage must be reported to the daimyo is not permitted marriage with a daughter of an *ashigaru*, the lord's groom, the lord's errand runner, or the lord's tea-room server, nor of a retainer of a subfief who must record his surname, nor with a woman who carries a *naijo* tag. However if, after his primary wife is divorced or after her death, he secretly takes a daughter of one of the above people as his concubine, and she gives birth to an heir or younger sons, she shall be permitted a "true mother" tag. Moreover, the various officials of the rank of commissioner of construction or lower, together with people receiving stipends of two hundred *koku* or more, as in the past, may not marry daughters of the above-named status.

Proviso: Even when a "true mother" tag is permitted, the procedure shall not be the same as for the primary wife. On her tag and in the register shall be entered her age, the name of her father, and the fact that the latter is attached to such-and-such office or is retainer of so-and-so (subfief holder). If her father is deceased she must record the name of her brother or some other head of the household.

5. Daughters of those in the *go-ichimon* rank down to castle-town samurai and lesser ranks, as well as attendant maids, shall not use the character for the honorific "o" above their names in either the register in the office of religious tag inspection or on their tags. This prohibition does not apply to such names as Okano, Onoe, or Oto.

6. Some daughters of commoners have been recorded as "joshi" of so-and-so, but henceforth they are instructed to be recorded as "*musume.*" This was strictly ordered by Lord Kyūma through Tabata Buemon on the nineteenth day, eighth month, twelfth year of Kansei (1800).

V. Regulations on the inspection of those without rank

1. Kameyama Isamu and Yamada Shozō were ordered to be without rank. Their tags and register were ordered to be inspected by the officer in charge of registration, and on their tags was to be recorded "office of the magistrate of tag inspection." As for investigative officials, those for the senior councilor group were ordered to serve concurrently as investigators [for the above two men]. Their attendants were ordered to record their ages and names and to note "attendant of so-and-so" on both their tags and in the register. Their female servants were ordered to record their ages and the term, "*tsukai-onna*." The above was ordered in the first month, sixth year of Temmei (1786).

VI. Regulations on the inspection of priests, mountain priests, and shrine personnel who have special status

1. A person who becomes a priest or mountain priest shall obtain a statement of confirmation from the office of the magistrate of temples and shrines.

Proviso: The mountain priest of the Tōzan school shall write, "Shugen sect," and the mountain priest of the Honzan school, "Tendai sect," on their tags.

2. The incumbent heads of the following seven temples, Nansen'in, Fukushōji, Daijōin, Jōkōmyōji, Ichijōin in Bōnotsu, Mirokuin of Kokubu, and Dairyūji shall be exempt from wearing tags because they have *chakuza* status at the time of the New Year audience with the *han* lord. When they retire tags are necessary.

3. The *chakuza* head priest of Senganji shall be seated next to the head priest of Ichijōin, as ordered in the eleventh month, eighth year of Tempō (1837).

4. The *chakuza* head priest of Jukokuji shall be seated next to the head priest of Dairyūji, as ordered in the ninth month, eleventh year of Bunka (1814) [*sic*, twelfth year of Bunka (1815), year of the boar].

5. The *chakuza* head priest of Fudankōin shall be seated next to the head priest of Fukushōji, as ordered in the ninth month, fourteenth year of Bunka (1817).

6. If the incumbent head of the Daijiji in Shibushi district is a priest of the [rank of] purple habit, he shall have *chakuza* status and

shall be exempt from wearing a tag. An incumbent who does not have *chakuza* status shall carry a tag.

7. A *chakuza* head priest, though he be from outside of the [Satsuma] domain, shall be exempt from wearing a tag as befits his status, and the explanation for the exemption shall be noted in the register.

8. For temples whose head priests are appointed with the approval of the daimyo, the written statement of the head priest shall suffice for purposes of inspection.

Proviso: All priests are exempt from recording their ages.

9. A priest from another domain who has charge of a temple in the *han* shall be treated the same as a Satsuma priest. Even if he does not preside over a temple, a priest who is permitted residence in Satsuma hereafter shall be issued a tag without exception, even though he does not request one personally. Moreover, a tag shall be issued to him when a statement from the head priest, testifying that the priest is from such-and-such domain and a disciple of such-and-such master is accompanied by an endorsement by the magistrate of temples and shrines. The above explanations and his religious sect affiliation shall be recorded on his tag and in the register.

Proviso: When the above priest leaves the domain the priest in charge of religious sect examination shall record this in the register for departing persons, submit [the register] to the investigative official and retrieve the [departing] priest's tag.

10. When a priest is on pilgrimage, at the time of tag inspection the priest in charge of the inspection shall record this in the register for departing persons, submit [the register] to the investigative official and retrieve the [departing priest's] old tag. When the latter returns to the domain and applies for a new tag he shall obtain a verifying statement from the head priest.

11. After the temple rank of the Renkōin of Ikumasan was proclaimed to be next to that of the Daijōin its head priest was assigned *chakuza* status regardless of whether he was of noble lineage or of common origin, as ordered in the first month, eleventh year of Bunsei (1828). Later, in the fifth month, second year of Tempō (1831), on the basis of a petition, the exemption from carrying a tag was extended to his successor.

12. All persons, including laity household members of the following eight temples, Umetanibō, Sakuraibō, Jippōbō, Matsuobō, Enokibō, Kadoyabō, Ikenobō, and Sugitanibō, each having separated from the house [of the head priest] of Renkōin of Ikumasan, shall be permitted the use of the surname, Kunigō. This surname shall be recorded on the tags and in the register. Moreover, priests of the above temples shall not use their temple names in their routine statements.

Proviso: Because of the lineage of the Renkōin its attendants are permitted the use of surnames.

13. Daughters of attendants of the Renkōin of Ikumasan shall have marriages equal with those of daughters of attendants of the *yoriai* rank, as ordered in the seventh month, seventh year of Bunsei (1824).

Proviso: *Naijo* [of the temple] also shall be equal with *naijo* of *yoriai*.

14. Attendants of the Renkōin of Ikumasan henceforth shall record on the margin, "member of the Renkōin, Kunigō," as ordered in the ninth month, seventh year of Bunsei (1824).

15. Shrine personnel and the laity at the Shōgū Hachiman shrine at Kokubu and the shrine personnel of Hachiman and of Nitta shrine who have been using surnames in the past shall continue to be on a reciprocal relationship for marriages with samurai who record their surnames and omit their ages.

Proviso: Servants of [shrine] officials, as in the previous inspection, shall write, "shrine messenger," on their tags and in the register.

16. Shrine personnel of Hirakiki in Ei district and members of the ten families of Ki, Nagayama, Aikō, Sakaki, Utsunomiya, Ueno, Inoue, Maruta, Nagakura, and Matsuyama are permitted as in the past to have reciprocal relationship for marriage with samurai who record their surnames and omit their ages.

17. As the Suwa Shrine of Kagoshima has been designated as a shrine especially revered by the *han* lord, the priests of its thirty households and their heirs, by special consideration of the daimyo, are hereby exempt from recording their ages. Their daughters may be married to castle-town samurai who do not require the lord's approval of marriage and to *gōshi* and *yoriki*, provided their ages

and social status are indicated on their tags and in the register. Regulations for second and younger sons shall be as in the past. These orders were issued in the eleventh month, seventh year of Bunsei (1824).

18. Since it is said that Ryukyuan priests of the Kagoshima Ryukyuan temple, Kōmyōji, and those residing in various districts came to Yamato [Kagoshima] to study without having removed their names from the original register [in Ryukyu], there is no need to issue them tags here.

19. The shrine of Shijūkusho Daimyōjin in Kōyama has had twenty-four shrine personnel households since ancient times. In recent years, however, due to impoverishment marriages appropriate to their social standing became difficult to arrange. In many cases families faced certain extinction because only single men remained. A petition was submitted, therefore, requesting permission for marriages on a reciprocal basis with rural townsmen, peasants, and temple-gate personnel within the district for a period of twenty years beginning with the year of the petition. Twice since the eleventh year of Kansei (1799) permission was granted as requested, but the periods having expired, again upon petition, permission was renewed as before for a twenty-year period beginning with the tenth year of Tempō (1839).

20. Honda Dewanokami and Inoue Suruganokami were granted the status of *chakuza* head priest. Upon request, they and their heirs were granted exemption from carrying tags, as of the order of the fifth month, second year of Kōka (1845).

21. It was ordered in the second month, fourth year of Kōka (1847) that the *chakuza* head priest of Han'nyain shall be seated next to the [head priest of] Renkōin of Ikumasan. Later, acting upon their petition, he and his heir were granted exemption from carrying a tag, as ordered in the eleventh month, fourth year of Kaei (1851).

VII. Regulations on tag inspection of ladies-in-waiting

1. Ladies-in-waiting who serve in the inner chamber, whether they be from families of samurai, or of *hitokerai*, townsmen, fishermen, peasants, or temple-gate personnel, shall have their tags kept in the office of the grand chamber. At the time of tag inspection the tags shall be submitted to the office of the magistrate of tag inspection. During their period of service to the daimyo they shall not need to carry tags.

Proviso: When they are dismissed from service the steward of the grand chamber shall issue them a statement of verification.

2. Similarly, ladies-in-waiting who are dismissed with completely satisfactory records, and who served with the title of *otsugi* or higher, though they be from families of *hitokerai* or of townsmen, fishermen, peasants, or temple-gate personnel, shall be permitted to marry samurai. At the time of their release the steward of the grand chamber shall issue them a written statement instructing them to request a new tag at their place of destination.

Proviso: They shall record their social status but not their ages. Maids who have served the han lord with the rank of *ohanshita* shall not marry samurai even if dismissed with completely satisfactory records.

3. Maids who are dismissed with not entirely satisfactory records, and who are from families of *hitokerai* or of townsmen, fishermen, peasants, or temple-gate personnel, shall not be permitted to

marry samurai. Regarding tags, the steward of the grand chamber shall issue them a written statement directing them to have new tags requested by the head of their original household. Daughters of samurai shall be governed by instructions at the time [of their release].

4. Women of lower social status, who have served [the *han* lord] as *otsugi* or higher position in the inner chamber and who are dismissed with completely satisfactory records, shall be permitted marriages with castle-town samurai and *gōshi*. In such cases they shall not be returned to their former social status, but people of samurai status shall take them in as members of their families. At the time of their release the steward of the grand chamber shall mention the above intention in each instance to those affected, and they are instructed that inclusion into a household shall be requested through their respective friends. If by chance a person finds it difficult to make such a request of a family, instructions will be issued by the steward of the grand chamber, as ordered in the sixth month, twelfth year of Bunka (1815).

VIII. Regulations on the [tag] inspection of *koban*, *shimban,* and *okoshōgumi*

1. When heirs of families, which have served for generations as *koban,* are too young to serve as guards, their retainers shall be recorded as *genin.* When they do enter service as guards [their retainers] shall be recorded as *kerai* and their surnames affixed in accordance with regulations.

2. Although a member of the *koban* rank may not adopt anyone of *gōshi* status, those who must petition for such action shall be placed in the *okoshōgumi* rank according to regulations. When a person's social status is so reduced his attendants shall receive *genin* tags.

3. The old tags shall be compared with the register for both men and women, and for those for whom there are no discrepancies tags shall be issued in conformance with past regulations.

Proviso: Those who have surnames shall not record, "same surname," but each person down to the youngest son shall write his surname.

4. When a child is born to a samurai a new tag shall be issued on the basis of written testimony that the child is truly his, attested by two neighborhood samurai in the case of Kagoshima, by the five-man association in the case of the district, and by two neighborhood *gōshi* in localities which have no five-man associations.

5. A person who leaves his own family to enter another house-

hold by adoption or marriage shall correct his tag with supporting documents from his former and current households.

6. When an heir dies or is sent away for adoption a petition is
made to permit moving up the second son to the position of heir,
and, in turn, another petition seeks permission to move up the
third and younger sons. Although in above situations petitions for
moving up second and younger sons have been granted [in the
past], hereafter when the heir dies or is sent away for adoption, the
petition for designating the heir shall be granted as in current
practice, but the third and younger sons shall not be moved up.
However, in the above situations, if there are second and third sons
to be moved up in a branch family of the Shimazu clan or in a
family of good lineage, a petition for moving up sons may be submitted as in the past if the change of status permits [these sons] the
presentation of gifts to the daimyo. If the change of status does not
allow the presentation of gifts to the daimyo, other than for the
heir, a petition for moving up boys may not be submitted, and
they shall remain in the positions to which they were born. If a
son, having been born as heir of a family which does not have the
status for presenting gifts to the lord, is sent away for adoption but
returns because of a change in situation, he shall be reinstated as
the eldest son of his original family. If later he requests permission
to establish a branch household, he shall be given the status of second son in various matters concerning the main family. While the
rules for moving up sons are the same as above, if second and
younger sons are sent away for adoption, but they return because
of a change in situation, naturally they shall be returned to their
previous positions in the family. When the heir or younger son of
a family, whose status permits the presentation of gifts to the daimyo, goes away for adoption, and after the other boys have been
moved up, he returns because of a change in situation, he shall not
be assigned to his former position, but he shall be reinstated in his
original family with the status of last son. If he petitions to establish a branch household, in various matters he shall have the same
status as that of the last son of the family. However, if the boys had
not been moved up to second and third son positions, they may
be moved up to these positions after the change in situation, as
decreed in the fourth month, eighth year of An'ei (1779).

Proviso: The above instructions shall apply also to *gōshi,* and the standings of all sons in the family shall be according to past regulations.

7. When the heir dies or is sent away for adoption a petition is made to designate the second son as heir. However, even though the family status may permit a petition to move up third and younger sons, since there may be numerous [brothers] below the second son, henceforth all [brothers] below the second son shall remain in the standing to which they were born and they shall not be permitted to move up. According to this regulation, for ex-ample, if the second son dies before his first audience with the daimyo, the third son shall have his audience as the third son and he shall present gifts to the daimyo as the third son. Of course, re-gardless of his standing in the family, when a petition is made to designate him as heir, this shall be governed as in the past, as pro-claimed in the fourth month, eleventh year of Kansei (1799).

8. In a household in which the adopted son becomes its head, when tags are received all children of the adoptive parents shall write in the character for "adoptive," such as "adoptive elder sis-ter," "adoptive younger sister," or "adoptive such-and-such."

Proviso: If the adoptive parents take in a foster child they must write "foster child so-and-so of foster father so-and-so."

9. Samurai whose marriage need not be reported to the lord, *yoriki* of various groups, and *gōshi,* may marry the daughters of *ashigaru,* of grooms, of the lord's errand runners, and of the lord's teahouse attendants as well as daughters of samurai retainers [of subfief holders], daughters of persons who record their surnames, and women who carry *naijo* tags. However, the "wife" tag shall not be prepared as in the past. On her tag the wife shall record her age, and on both her tag and in the register she shall record her father's name, to which office he is attached, or whom he serves as a retainer. If the father is deceased she must record the name of her brother or of some other [head] member of the family.

Proviso: The above provision does not apply to a *naijo* who did not record the fact during the previous inspection either on her tag or in the register, even though she may have a statement of release that she served as *naijo.*

10. When a samurai of *koban* or *shimban* rank has a child by his

concubine he shall apply to the office of the magistrate of tag inspection for a certificate of permit for obtaining a "true son" tag by submitting his own report, a verifying statement by two samurai from his neighborhood, and an endorsement written for the applicant by the office of *ōbangashira*.

11. When a similar situation occurs to a member of the *okoshōgumi* rank the same procedure as above shall be followed with a submission of a report by the person involved, a supporting statement by two neighborhood samurai, to which would be pasted notes by the head of the *kogumi,* and a final confirmation by the chief of the *okoshōgumi* guards.

12. When a similar situation occurs to *yoriki* of various units the same procedure as above shall be followed with the submission of his own report, supporting statements by two neighborhood samurai, to which would be pasted an endorsement by the sponsor if the case involves a *yoriki* assigned to the bureau of weapons, and by the *kogashira* if the case involves a *yoriki* assigned to the daimyo's grand chamber, and a final confirmation by the supervisory chief.

Proviso: When a *gōshi* petitions for a "true child" tag for a child born by his permanent maid he shall submit his own report together with endorsements by his five-man association, his unit chief, and the *gōshi* elder, and a final confirmation by the *jitō*, which are pasted to the report.

13. A daughter of a person whose tag is that of a member of a castle-town samurai household and whose samurai lineage is certain, shall be permitted to marry [a samurai] whose marriage does not require a report to the lord.

14. Persons with tags of samurai households or even of households of *ashigaru,* of the lord's grooms, or of the lord's errand runners, if they record their surnames, are of the same status as *ashigaru,* the lord's grooms, the lord's errand runners, and the lord's teahouse attendants; and if their lineages are verified their daughters may marry those whose marriages do not need to be reported to the lord.

Proviso: Daughters of the above who do not have surnames shall not be permitted to marry samurai. However, if a child of a samurai is born by one of the above women, upon investigation, a "true mother" tag shall be permitted.

15. Daughters of shrine personnel and temple-gate personnel are not permitted to marry samurai.

16. Daughters of shrine personnel, temple-gate personnel, townsmen, fishermen, and peasants, who, for some reason, were permitted to marry [castle-town] samurai or *gōshi,* and who received "wife" tags before the inspection of the second year of Gembun (1737), need not record their ages on their tags. However, they must record on their tags and in the register the names of their own fathers and such explanations as where their fathers serve as shrine personnel, temple-gate personnel, townsmen, fishermen, or peasants. If the father is deceased the name and social status of a brother or other head of the household shall be recorded.

17. The above regulations shall apply to a daughter of the above who has received a tag as samurai wife, but whose husband has died and who at the moment is carrying a "grandmother" or "true mother" tag.

18. The above regulations shall apply to a daughter of the above who has married a [samurai] of dependent status and received a wife tag, but who is made a foster daughter by the family of the husband immediately after his death, which occurred before they had children.

19. Daughters of the above, who were married after the last tag inspection [1737] but who have not yet obtained wife tags, shall verify their social status and submit a statement of confirmation by the magistrate of accounting. The statements shall be ascertained, the revisions shall be made in accordance with the above regulations, and the tags shall be issued.

20. Even daughters of the above categories who, having been made concubines [of castle-town samurai or *gōshi*] and having given birth to children, request "true mother" tags shall all be issued tags in accordance with the above procedures.

21. Since it is forbidden for castle-town samurai and *gōshi* to marry daughters of the lower classes or to adopt children of the lower classes, great care shall be taken in the inspection.

22. Wives and children of *gōshi* who have been appointed as castle-town samurai shall have their old tags checked, and if there are no discrepancies, the said tags shall be amended. For those who request tags for inclusion of their parents into their households,

these tags shall be issued on the basis of supporting documents written by the *gōshi* elder and various other officials of their original district. On the tags shall be written the side notations "of such-and-such household" and "parents of so-and-so." Other brothers and relatives who hold tags of the [above] household shall be issued tags from the original district.

23. The above procedure shall apply for revising the tags of the wife and children of a person who has been appointed to be a [castle-town] samurai. When parents request tags for inclusion in the above households, tags shall be issued as petitioned upon the submission of verifying statements by the supervisory chief in the case of Kagoshima, by the *gōshi* elder and various other officials in the case of a *gōshi*, and in accordance with past regulations in the case of a retainer of a private domain. Moreover, on both tags and in the register the names of the parents shall be included. If the parents' petition is denied, their tags shall be marked as in the past. As it is strictly forbidden to give samurai tags additionally to brothers and relatives who hold tags of the [above] household, their tags shall be prepared and issued in the same way as in the past.

24. If a person unavoidably must petition for a tag for new admission into a samurai household, such as for a relative or a child brought along by his wife, he shall write a detailed explanation of the situation, bring various statements by relatives and neighbors, and an endorsement by their respective supervisory chief, which are pasted to the report, and present them to the office of the magistrate for tag inspection, where the matter shall be investigated.

Proviso: A person from the district shall bring statements by relatives, neighbors, and the five-man association which are endorsed by the *gōshi* elder and countersigned by the *jitō* by pasting on their statements to the original statements, and a person from a private domain shall bring documents as in the past, and these shall be submitted to the office of the magistrate for tag inspection, where they shall be carefully studied. The old register will be examined to ascertain where the person had been located at the time of the previous inspection, to which household he belonged, and what type of tag he had obtained, and these facts shall be entered in the register. When the investigation is completed, the information shall be abstracted and submitted in a separate book.

25. When a daughter of a [castle-town] samurai, a *gōshi,* or a commoner, due to some wrong committed by her parent, is assigned as a maid to a *gōshi* and she gives birth to a child, the request for information on procedures for obtaining an identification tag shall be directed to the office of the magistrate for tag inspection, where an investigation shall be made.

26. When tags of castle-town samurai were lost, worm-eaten, burned, or defaced, they have been submitting petitions with proper endorsements and countersignatures pasted on to the original petitions. Henceforth, however, they shall personally submit their papers at once to the office of tag inspection, and as for the various supervisory chiefs, they need only be informed of the situation. However, the procedure for "true child" and "true mother" tags shall be as in the past.

Proviso: In the same situation as above, the *gōshi* shall submit to the office of tag inspection his own report with endorsements by the five-man association, the *yokome,* the chief of his group, and the *gōshi* elders pasted on to the report. However, the *jitō* need only be informed.

27. Castle-town samurai and *gōshi* who request leave to become subretainers henceforth shall be forbidden to return to their former status. If they leave their status permanently, they shall be given a tag assigning them to the household of a relative, and they shall write a side notation on their tags and in the register, "formerly a relative of so-and-so." Moreover, they shall remove their surnames [from the register] and their ages shall be recorded.

28. When the wife of a castle-town samurai or *gōshi* is divorced and she is sent away with her daughter, and the household to which she returns as daughter is unable to support them, or if the girl stays in a household for any other reason and the household finds it difficult to support the child, or if the second husband of the divorced mother dies, making it difficult to support the child, or if for some unavoidable reason [the girl] is supported by some other household, a petition shall be submitted for a change of household indicating a desire for a tag which assigns the child to such-and-such person. If upon investigation nothing wrong is found in her background, the tag shall be issued as requested.

IX. Regulations on the inspection of tags of *yoriki* attached to various units and of *ashigaru* and the like who are attached to various offices

1. When a person is appointed one-generation *yoriki* attached to some unit, a tag shall be issued him on the basis of a written statement by the lord's steward. His one-generation *yoriki* status shall be recorded on his tag and in the register.

2. If the above person submits a petition requesting that members of his original household be given tags for his [new status] household, the inclusion into the household shall be permitted on the basis of a written statement by the supervisory chief. Both tags and register shall reflect the person's [new] status. Later, upon the death of the head of family, the tags shall be corrected to their original forms, and they shall be carefully examined so there will be no confusion.

3. As for the marriage of the person who has been appointed to the above position, he may take as his wife a woman whose status does not permit marriage with castle-town samurai. However, she must record her social status.

4. In the above situation, if he should die after he has taken a wife, or after they have children, the latter shall be issued tags denoting their former *ashigaru* status.

Proviso: Daughters of the above [*yoriki*] are not permitted to marry those who must report their marriages to the daimyo.

5. *Ashigaru,* the lord's groom, the lord's errand runner, and the

lord's teahouse attendant, shall record their surnames and their ages on their tags and in the register.

6. The issuance or withdrawal of tags for *ashigaru,* the lord's errand runner, the lord's groom, and the lord's teahouse attendant, shall be on the basis of a written statement by their [respective] supervisory chief.

7. The tags of the above-named persons' wives, daughters, maid servants, and man servants, shall be corrected on the basis of written statements submitted by their respective sponsor.

8. When a woman who has a maid-servant tag of the household of an *ashigaru,* the lord's errand runner, the lord's groom, or the lord's teahouse attendant, changes her tag to that of a wife, an investigation shall be made on the basis of a written statement by the supervisory chief.

9. People who are attached to various offices shall record their surnames and ages on their tags and in the register, and they shall be permitted a reciprocal relationship for marriages with those of *ashigaru* and lower rank.

10. Unskilled workers attached to the above various offices shall be permitted to adopt or marry anyone without surnames from whatever location.

11. People attached to the various offices shall not marry [into the status of] castle-town samurai, *gōshi,* or *yoriki,* as ordered in the sixth month, seventh year of Bunsei (1824).

12. The lord's palanquin bearers, carriers of the lord's travel chests, and the lord's cooks, who have served him satisfactorily throughout several years, on the basis of the above factors may be permitted the use of a surname for the lifetime of the individual alone.

X. Regulations on [tag] inspection of *gōshi* and *gōshi* who are guards in various districts

1. No household shall be established in the register of tag inspection excepting those which are listed in the register for *gōshi* land stipends. A check shall be made to insure that the listing of households will be the same as in the register for land stipends which is submitted annually to the office of commissioner of land stipends.

2. A *gōshi* who has his own son is forbidden from adopting an heir. However, if succession by his son is difficult due to [the latter's] chronic ailment or disability, at that time a petition shall be submitted, and upon its receipt by the *jitō* adoption may be permitted; but the tag shall be issued after careful examination of the situation.

3. A *gōshi* who lives in a different district shall receive his tag from his district of origin. He shall obtain from his district of origin a written statement certifying how many people received tags for his household, and this shall be submitted to the inspecting officer at the district of present residence.

4. A daughter of a *gōshi* who has married into a household category of subretainer, shrine personnel, or temple-gate personnel which requires that ages be recorded, shall indicate her age on her tag just as do the other members of her [new] household.

5. Children of *rōnin* who reside in various districts, and of *ashigaru* of Ōmura district are permitted marriage reciprocity with

74

gōshi within their own district, and they may receive wife-tags. They are not permitted to marry anyone outside of their district.

Proviso: There is no objection to male and female servants going back and forth to other disticts.

6. Koshikijima, being an island, is different from other villages in that no one comes in. Thus *gōshi* have difficulty arranging marriages within their status. Consequently they are allowed marriage reciprocity with people throughout the island who are of the categories of peasants, fishermen, and shrine personnel. Tags shall be corrected on the basis of testimony by the local officials.

Proviso: Their ages and social status shall be recorded in accordance with regulations.

7. *Gōshi* of Shibushi district who are guards at the frontier roads in Shinchi, Kawarada, Bishagano, and Ōkawachi, being located in the mountains, have no one to marry. Thus they are permitted marriages with daughters of townsmen, peasants, shrine personnel, and temple-gate personnel. Of course, this should not be construed as a precedent.

Proviso: Their ages and family background shall be recorded in accordance with regulations.

8. A frontier guard post having been established at Nihonmatsu in Tanoura in Shibushi district, two men have been transferred there for regular duty. The above two men are permitted marriages with [daughters of] townsmen, peasants, shrine personnel, and temple-gate personnel, as proclaimed in the eighth year of An'ei (1779).

Proviso: Their ages and social status shall be recorded in accordance with regulations.

9. Because the four [frontier] districts of Takaoka, Kuraoka, Aya, and Mukasa have few women, *gōshi* have difficulty arranging marriages proper to their status. In addition, because of poverty they find it even more difficult to arrange marriages with people in the inner districts [surrounding the castle-town]. Due to these various obstacles some lineages have died out in the course of events. Consequently, in the past when [a *gōshi*] requested a "true child" tag for a child born by a woman day laborer, though contrary to law, the request was granted. However, in the fifth year of Gembun (1740) it was proclaimed that because it violated the law

permission no longer would be granted thereafter. On the other hand, it was ordered that due to the above-stated shortage of women in these places if a petition is made for marriage with daughters of townsmen or peasants, upon official investigation, permission may be granted. A person granted such permission, on the basis of a verifying statement by the *jitō* shall obtain a "true child" tag for a child born to him.

Proviso: A perosn who divorces such a wife shall report this to the office of the magistrate for tag insepction or sometimes to the office of accounting [*han*]. If later he contracts a similar marriage he shall again report in the above manner. Of course, the recording of age and social status shall be in accordance with regulations.

10. The village of Kamiya of Nojiri district, being located on the border of another domain, frequently must summon a number of men on sudden notice whenever there are runaways. Thus if the number of *gōshi* gradually decreases this service for the daimyo would be adversely affected. However, being located in the heart of the mountains in addition to being very poor, they are unable to arrange marriages with their peers, and there are only single men around. Therefore upon request they shall be permitted to marry daughters of peasants and rural townsmen in the districts of Nojiri and Kobayashi, but this shall not be construed as a precedent.

Proviso: Age and social status shall be recorded in accordance with regulations.

11. *Gōshi* of Kobayashi district who serve as guards at Kiuragi, being located away from the district administrative seat and in the heart of the mountains, have been unable to marry daughters of their peers. Since their location borders on another domain and thus constitutes a special case, henceforth upon request as in the past, they are permitted to marry daughters of townsmen and peasants within their district.

Proviso: In addition to permitting the above marriages, again upon request, permission was granted in the ninth year of Hōreki (1759) for marriages with daughters of rural townsmen and peasants in the districts of Suki and Kakutō. Of course, age and social status shall be recorded in accordance with regulations.

12. After a person has been given a one-generation appoint-

ment as *gōshi* he shall be allowed to marry a woman whose status does not allow her to marry a castle-town samurai. However she must record her social status.

13. *Gōshi* who reside in Hetsuka in the district of Sata, being removed in the mountains about four or five *ri* from their district administrative seat, and being especially poor, are unable to arrange marriages with women from other districts, not to speak of their own district. Upon their petition, in the seventh year of Bunsei (1824) for a period of ten years hence, they were permitted to take in by marriage the daughters of peasants, but the period expired in the fourth year of Tempō (1833).

14. In the case of a *gōshi* placed under the charge of another samurai, unless the fact that he is assigned to such-and-such a family is recorded in the register, there is the possibility of confusion in later years. Therefore, henceforth the above fact shall be recorded both on the tag and in the register, as proclaimed in the twelfth month, seventh year of Bunsei (1824).

15. Because Momiki Heiuemon and Futami Kyūemon, *gōshi* of Takaoka, are regular guards assigned to the major barrier at Sarukawa, their servants, by the lord's special consideration, are permitted to marry daughters of peasants.

XI. Regulations on the inspection of tags of sub-retainers and of servants of castle-town samurai

1. Daughters of subretainers who record their surnames and are serving samurai of *koban* rank, and daughters of those with tags of servants of castle-town samurai shall in no case be allowed to have tags denoting "wife of castle-town samurai." However, when they are made concubines and they give birth to children, upon investigation they shall be permitted "true mother" tags.

Proviso: The above shall apply also to *gōshi*.

2. Concerning the manner of recording surnames of subretainers, although regulations have been followed in the past, some writing downwards [i.e., in the same column] and others along the side [of their personal names], it is ordered that everyone shall write downwards, and surnames shall be so recorded. Even a person who has no surname but is allowed one by his master shall record this surname in the same way as for the other subretainers. Moreover, a subretainer who enters a household which does not have the status which permits its subretainers surnames, shall not record his surname as in the case of the other subretainers.

3. The entry or departure of attendants, maid servants, and male servants shall be investigated with verifying documents of both [new and old masters].

4. The following attendants of Hongō Sakuzaemon have lived in the four villages of Takajō district, Morokata county: Kuroki Kitarō, Futami Kinzō, Kuroki Gengorō, Nagamine Sesuke, Futa-

mi Kingorō, Futami Hansuke, Nagamine Shichizaemon, Futami Jin'uemon, Inoue Han'uemon, Nagamine Gorōzaemon, and Inoue Chūbei. Because they are guards at by-roads, upon petition they shall be permitted to marry daughters of rural townsmen and peasants.

5. Attendants of those who have served as hereditary *koban* shall record on their tags their ages, surnames, and "attendant of so-and-so." Maid servants shall be recorded as *"gejo."* Attendants of those who serve as one-generation *koban* or as hereditary *shimban* shall not record surnames.

Proviso: As there are attendants who reside in the districts and who obtain their tags there, care shall be taken to avoid mistakes.

6. For those who serve as *okoshōgumi*, whose ancestors served in a high office, or held the post of *jitō*, or were of good family lineage, their attendants nevertheless shall omit their surnames and record themselves as *"genin"* (servant).

Proviso: The above applies also to attendants who reside in the districts.

7. Servants of castle-town samurai, being without surnames, shall be recorded as *"genin"* even though heretofore they may have had *"kerai"* or *"hikan"* marked on their tags.

8. Okobira Kyūshirō has been stationed as a guard at Iino. Upon his petition his attendants shall be permitted to marry daughters of peasants and rural townsmen.

9. The servants of Okobira Rokurōbei, who is stationed as a guard at the border at Iino, are all without wives due to the remoteness of the location. Upon petition they are permitted marriage reciprocity with rural townsmen and with peasants, as proclaimed in the seventh month, first year of Kyōwa (1801).

10. All servants of subretainers shall have *"genin"* tags.

11. If daughters of peasants, [rural] townsmen, fishermen, shrine personnel, and temple-gate personnel are placed on term employment with castle-town samurai on the basis of verifying statements by their respective supervisory chiefs, and during this period they have liaison with other people, the children born of such relationships shall be assigned to the employer.

Proviso: If, while husband and wife are employed on a term basis with a permit, a child is born to them, the child shall be assigned to the employer. If the husband is employed on a term basis while his wife remains in their home district, and a child is born to them, the child shall be assigned to the mother. If the wife is employed on a term basis while her husband remains in their home district, and if the above wife bears her husband's child, the child shall be assigned to the employer. If the father of the child, who is assigned to the employer, is a peasant, [rural] townsman, fisherman, or a member of shrine or temple-gate personnel, the child shall be given a servant tag. If the father is the attendant of a castle-town samurai and has a surname, the child also shall record his surname the same as his father. However, if the employer is not of a status which permits his servant to have a surname, the child also shall be without surname. If the husband is under term employment and he has relations with a maid servant, a child resulting therefrom shall be assigned as above.

XII. Regulations on the inspection of tags of Shinto priests, Shinto priestesses, priests of local deities, blind lutists, and temple-gate personnel

1. In the time of Inoue Yamatonokami, the chief priest of Suwa shrine at Fukugazako went to Kyoto and was initiated into the funeral rites and the ceremonies of Shintoism by the Yoshida family. Since then only those who are serving as Shinto priests shall record "Shinto priest" on their tags and in the register. People of their households, as in the past, shall indicate their religious sect, as ordered in the fifth month, first year of Kyōwa (1801).

2. Shrine personnel who are assigned as shrine priests shall be examined on the basis of verifying statements written by the magistrate for temples and shrines.

3. When daughters of shrine personnel in Kagoshima marry, or when male or female servants depart or enter [the household of shrine personnel], their names shall be removed from the register on the basis of written statements with endorsements by their supervisory chiefs pasted to them.

4. All shrine priests shall record their surnames and ages on their tags. They are not permitted to marry samurai.

5. When shrine personnel or temple-gate personnel permanently withdraw their tags to [go to] other places, they shall obtain a verifying statement from the office of the magistrate for temples and shrines.

6. When daughters of the above people marry, or when their

male or female servants leave the household, they shall be investigated on the basis of written testimony as directed by past regulations.

7. When shrine personnel of peasant status are appointed to be Shintō priests, or if they establish branch households, they shall be examined on the basis of verifying statements by the chief priest of Suwa shrine in Kagoshima.

8. Servants with no surnames who are serving temple and shrine personnel shall be recorded as *"genin."* They shall not be recorded as *"hikan," "kerai,"* or *"uchi."*

9. Priestesses of Kagoshima, regardless of their social status, during their period of service in the shrine, shall record their ages and write a side notation both on their tags and in the register, "so-and-so person of such-and-such place"; and they shall be placed under the jurisdiction of the office for temples and shrines in Kagoshima. Of course, if their request to withdraw from their office as *naishi* [priestess] is approved, they may marry anyone they wish within the appropriate status.

10. Since the temple-gate personnel of the Yōshun'in temple of Yamada district in Shira county were impoverished and unable to arrange marriages appropriate to their station, marriage reciprocity was permitted for a certain period beginning with the twelfth year of Bunka (1815) with rural townsmen and peasants within the same district and with rural townsmen, peasants, and *hitokerai* of the districts of Chōsa, Kajiki, Mizobe, and Kamō. This period having expired, permission was renewed as in the past for a period of ten years beginning with the eighth year of Tempō (1837) and [the renewal] expired in the third year of Kōka (1846).

11. All shrine priestesses in administrative districts and in private domains, including those who are of *gōshi,* attendant, or lower status, personally requested to serve concurrently in their positions. Therefore, with the exception of the wife of a shrine priest, for other shrine priestesses the tag inspection shall be in accordance with their social status. During the period of their service in the shrine they shall enter a side notation on their tags and in the register that they are priestesses of such-and-such shrine in such-and-such place. If the priestess has a husband and she gives birth to a child during the period of her service with the

shrine, the child shall be given a tag for inclusion in her husband's household. Moreover, if she becomes a priestess before she is married, there is no objection to her getting married later, and a child born to her shall be given a tag in the manner stipulated above.

12. As for priests of local deities, blind priests, and [blind] lutists, in every case their social status shall be investigated and entered on their tags and in the register. Tags issued to their children shall have a side notation with the same social status entry as for the father.

13. Temple-gate personnel of the Nansen'in shall record both on their tags and in the register the name of their shop as their household name.

14. Temple-gate personnel of all temples shall be without surnames as provided in previous regulations.

Proviso: Temple-gate agents of the Fukushōji temple shall have surnames as provided in previous regulations. Temple-gate agents of the six temples of Daijōin, Jōkōmyōji, Dairyūji, Kōkokuji, Nanrinji, and Myōkokuji shall record their ages and surnames on their tags and in the register as heretofore.

15. Since the three families of the temple-gate agents of Fukushōji temple have not been granted entry into samurai units, no one from among the rank of *okoshōgumi* may be adopted by these families. Since these families unavoidably will be terminated if this situation continues they have petitioned to be admitted into [samurai] units. However, if orders were issued as petitioned, they would be contrary to the daimyo's long-standing objective and the lineages of these families would be blurred. Therefore it is difficult to issue the order as petitioned. On the other hand, if these families are allowed to die off it would become even more difficult to fulfill the daimyo's will. Hence these three families, regardless of their social status, shall be permitted by the daimyo's consideration to adopt children from among *gōshi* and various groups of *yoriki,* as ordered in the fourth month, eighth year of Kansei (1796).

16. If men and women among the temple-gate personnel marry attendants of castle-town samurai or people attached to various offices and they do not correct their tags, it would appear that

they are [actually] employed as day laborers to pay off the interest on their debts. Children born by them, therefore, shall be assigned to temple-gate [status], and both parties shall be levied a fine of one *kammon* each.

Proviso: After the fine is levied, even though they state that there was nothing wrong with their marriage, their petition shall be denied.

17. A separate book shall be prepared for the tag inspection register for temple-gate personnel and shrine personnel.

18. Since shrine personnel of Takaoka, Aya, Kuraoka, and Mukasa districts have difficulty arranging marriages among the same shrine households, upon their request, they shall be permitted to marry daughters of peasants and rural townsmen of these four districts. They shall submit a request each time for such marriages. Moreover, if they wish marriages as above because they are divorced or because they wish to establish a branch family, they shall submit a petition as stipulated above.

19. The following twenty-one families of temple-gate personnel of the Fukushōji, being of good lineage, shall be permitted to have their surnames recorded, and this privilege is extended to include only their heirs and retired heads of families: Saigō, Aira, Iimure, Matsumoto, Satō, Maeda, Zushi, Miyazato, Somekawa, Nishida, Sameshima, Yamanouchi, Suzuki, Higashi, Taneda, the two Ōyama families, Ikeda, Miyahara, Matsushita, and Nagata.

20. Concerning shrine priests of Kakutō district, Kuroki Tachū, who is head priest of Ninomiya Gennō shrine of the same district, and family members of shrine priests in the same district, formerly there were seven families, but now only four remain, of which three have no married men. These families are unable to arrange marriages appropriate to their status within their district or with neighboring districts. If this situation continues, inevitably the families of priests will gradually die out. Consequently, upon their petition, they shall be permitted to marry the daughters of peasants and rural townsmen of the districts of Kakutō, Kobayashi, and Iino, as granted in the first year of Temmei (1781).

21. Shrine personnel of the shrines of Sano Gongen and Higashi Gozaisho in Takahara district, upon their petition, were granted permission to take into their families by marriage or adoption

[sons and daughters of] peasants and rural townsmen who resided within their own district [of Takahara] and in the districts of Kobayashi and Takasaki. Since the twelfth year of Kansei (1800) from time to time permission was granted for definite periods. The preceding period having expired, on the eighth year of Tempō (1837) for a period of twenty years thereafter, permission was again granted for marriage reciprocity with rural townsmen, peasants, and temple-gate personnel within the said district of Takahara and in the districts of Takasaki and Kobayashi.

22. Temple-gate personnel of the Jintokuin and Shakujōin of Takahara district, upon petition, were granted permission for marriages with peasants and rural townsmen residing within their own district, of course, and also within the districts of Takasaki and Kobayashi. Since the twelfth year of Kansei (1800) this permission was renewed from time to time for definite periods. The preceding period having expired, once again in the eighth year of Tempō (1837) permission was granted as in the past for a period of twenty years thereafter.

23. Temple-gate personnel of the Shingakuji of Chōsa district, being poor, have been unable to arrange marriages in distant areas, and unavoidably they have requested permanent leave. Gradually these families have declined, and at the present time there are only a few men and women left. If the present situation continues, in a few years the families will have died off. Consequently they have petitioned for an order permitting them marriage reciprocity with people in the categories of peasants, rural townsmen, fishermen, and *hitokerai*. Marriage reciprocity with rural townsmen, fishermen, and *hitokerai* shall be permitted for the time being as of the seventh month, sixth year of Temmei (1786).

24. Temple-gate personnel of the Ganjōji of Chōsa district, being gradually reduced in numbers, upon their petition, have been granted permission for the time being to marry rural townsmen, fishermen, and [*hito*]*kerai* as proclaimed in the twelfth month, sixth year of Meiwa (1769).

25. Servants of the temple of Shingakuji of Chōsa district, being located in an out-of-the-way place and there being few people of like status, upon their petition, have been granted permission for the time being for marriage reciprocity with people in

the categories of peasants, rural townsmen, fishermen, and *hito-kerai*, as proclaimed in the twelfth month, year of the ox [sixth year of Meiwa, 1769].

26. Temple-gate personnel of the Busshōin of Takarabe district, though poor from the beginning, have become even more impoverished in recent years. Being unable to arrange marriages appropriate to their station with people in other districts, the men are all without wives, and their number has gradually been reduced. Consequently, upon their request, they were permitted marriage reciprocity with peasants and rural townsmen within the district as of the fourth month, second year of Tempō (1831) for a period of ten years thereafter. The period expired in the eleventh year of Tempō (1840).

27. Temple-gate personnel of the Shin'yūji of Yoshida district in Kagoshima county, being few in number and all the men being without wives, submitted a petition for marriage reciprocity with peasants of their district and of other districts. From time to time they were granted this permission for definite periods, but the last period having expired, again, upon their petition, they were granted permission in the second year of Kōka (1845) as in the past for twenty years thereafter.

28. Temple-gate personnel of Hokkedakeji of Takaoka district, being reduced to a small number of people, were unable to arrange marriages appropriate to their station. Upon their petition, they were granted permission for marriage reciprocity with servants of *gōshi*, rural townsmen, and peasants, as of the fourth year of Tempō (1833) for twenty years thereafter.

29. Temple-gate personnel and servants of the Hōfukuji of Kawanabe district, being generally impoverished, were unable to arrange marriages appropriate to their stations. Upon their petition, they were granted permission for marriage reciprocity with peasants and rural townsmen of their district and of the districts of Taniyama, Chiran, Kaseda, Yamada of Kawanabe county, Ata, Tabuse, and Izaku, as of the tenth year of Tempō (1839) for twenty years thereafter.

30. Temple-gate personnel of the Gyokusenji of the same district [i.e., Kawanabe], being generally impoverished, have been unable to arrange marriages appropriate to their station. Upon

their petition, they were granted permission for marriage reciprocity with peasants and rural townsmen of their district and in the districts of Taniyama, Chiran, Kaseda, Yamada of Kawanabe county, Ata, Tabuse, and Izaku as of the tenth year of Tempō (1839) for twenty years thereafter.

XIII. Regulations on the inspection of tags of the people of Naishirogawa

1. It is reported that at present there are only seventeen clan names among the people of Naishirogawa. Thus, the clan name shall be recorded in each case with one character written above the personal name. Of course, these are not surnames, and the social status shall be as in the past. Moreover, Ri Tatsuba, Shin Jūen, Boku Shun'eki, and Shin Shunshō were granted the status of *gōshi* of Ijūin in former years. These four men were granted the status of *gōshi* to include their heirs, but their second and younger sons shall retain their past standings. They are allowed the use of one character each to designate their clans because these are characters which they had in their home country [Korea]. Thus in each case one character is permitted to record their clan names.

2. Daughters of peasants, fishermen, rural townsmen and others shall be permitted to marry into the families in Naishirogawa. It is strictly forbidden for residents of Naishirogawa to leave for other areas by marriage.

Proviso: A woman who takes her leave after having served the daimyo fully satisfactorily in the grand inner chamber with the rank of *otsugi* or higher shall be permitted to marry anyone at the daimyo's discretion. On such an occasion she shall be issued a tag on the basis of a verifying statement written by the steward of the grand chamber.

3. The four households of Ri Tatsuba, Shin Jūen, Boku Shun'-eki, and Shin Shunshō should arrange adoptions and marriages on a reciprocal basis among those of equal status. However, because they are few in number, those who have difficulty making arrangements which are appropriate to their social standing shall be permitted to arrange adoptions and marriages with residents of Naishirogawa with good lineages.

4. Residents of Naishirogawa who were transferred to Kasano-hara in Kanoya district shall be governed by the above provisions in matters concerning their reciprocal relationship for marriages and adoptions and entrance into and departures from the community. The inspection shall be carried out accordingly.

5. In consideration of Boku Taijun's several decades of service as Korean interpreter, he and his heirs in the succeeding two generations shall be given the rank of *gōshi* of Ijūin district, as ordered in the tenth month, fifth year of Bunsei (1822).

XIV. Regulations on the inspection of tags of the townsmen of Kagoshima

1. Persons who leave the three town districts of Kamimachi, Shimomachi, and Nishidamachi of Kagoshima city to be married or adopted in fishing villages shall be required to obtain a verifying statement written by the town magistrate.

Proviso: The departure of female and male servants to other areas shall be governed by past procedures.

2. Concerning the above persons, when entry or departure [for marriages and adoptions] takes place on a reciprocal basis within the three town districts, the verifying statements shall be written by the chief town official of the year and by the five-man association.

3. When the above entry or departure takes place within one of the three *machi* [of Kagoshima], verifying statements from the five-man association are required.

4. When residents of Kamimachi, Shimomachi, and Nishidamachi of Kagoshima leave their district for fishing villages for the purpose of marriage or adoption, or when residents of fishing villages for the same reasons enter the three town districts of Kagoshima, they shall apply at the offices of the town magistrate and the maritime magistrate, and they shall have their names withdrawn from their original place of tag registration on the basis of verifying statements written by the two magistrates.

Proviso: Marriage reciprocity shall be permitted among townsmen who reside in the above three town districts, fishing villagers
who are under the supervision of the two maritime magistrates
[located at Tempōzan and at Gumisaki], and temple-gate personnel of Nansen'in and Nanrinji and of the temples of Daijiji,
Daiseiin, Kaitokuji, and Eitaiji in Shibushi district, because these
people provide maritime corvée service. Others who do not provide such service shall not be permitted the above type of marriage
relationship.

5. Among Kagoshima townsmen only the *myōzu* are all permitted the use of surnames, and members of their families also shall
record their surnames both on their tags and in the register.

6. Certainly the residents of the three town districts of Kagoshima, but also the people from the several [administrative] districts,
who have been elevated by the daimyo to samurai status in consideration of their voluntary contributions of money, shall all be
granted the extension of their status to their successors in the next
two generations, as proclaimed in the tenth month, tenth year of
Bunsei (1827).

XV. Regulations on the tag inspection of peasants and rural townsmen

1. A female servant of a castle-town samurai, or of an attendant, or of temple-gate or shrine personnel, is permitted to marry into a peasant village. However, the district official shall have the statement of her master in making a report to the agricultural office; and her tag shall be corrected to that of a peasant wife on the basis of a certificate of the agricultural magistrate.

Proviso: If a person has taken a bride without correcting her "wife" tag despite the fact that such marriages are permitted as stated above, it would appear that she is employed as a day laborer to pay the interest on a loan. Consequently both parties shall be fined one *kammon* each, and children born by their union shall receive their tags from the peasant village. Even though the above parties petition that there was nothing wrong with their marriage, their petition shall be denied.

2. If a female servant of a castle-town samurai or of shrine or temple-gate personnel gives birth to a child by a peasant who is employed as a day laborer, the child shall receive the tag of the father's peasant household. Moreover, since the law was violated, in accordance with the law both parties shall be fined one *kammon* each.

3. Attendants of castle-town samurai, persons attached to various offices, shrine personnel, and temple-gate personnel, who enter peasant villages [by marriage or adoption] shall report to

the agricultural office and shall receive "peasant" tags on the basis of a certificate from the agricultural magistrate.

Proviso: Those who have been sold to peasants by samurai, *gōshi*, or anyone else, and who have certificates of the agricultural magistrate, even though they have not yet received [new] tags, shall be prohibited from returning to their former employers.

4. When the above-mentioned persons are ordered to become male or female servants of peasants, they shall receive "male servant" or "female servant" tags on the basis of a certificate of the agricultural magistrate. Moreover, in accordance with regulations, they shall bring from the office of original tag issue to their [new] destination a certificate of tag withdrawal. The old tags shall be verified and thereupon new tags shall be issued.

Proviso: It was proclaimed through the agency of Suekawa Shōgen in the fifth month, first year of Bunsei (1818) that a female servant of a *gōshi* and the male and female servants of peasants shall be differentiated by calling the former *"gōshi meshitsukai"* and the latter *"hyakushō meshitsukai."* Those who are permanently in the service of *gōshi* may be designated as in the past as *"genin"* or *"gejo."* A person who is assigned to [serve] a *gōshi* or peasant because of an offense henceforth shall be recorded as *"meshitsukai"* both on his tag and in the register.

5. If a child of a peasant, regardless of sex, is adopted by [another] peasant as his foster child, or if a child is brought along into the family by the wife of a peasant, it shall be reported to the agricultural office, and the child's name shall be removed from the original place of tag issue on the basis of a certificate issued by the agricultural magistrate.

6. When a peasant wishes to divide his household, the agricultural magistrate shall permit the establishment of a branch household on the basis of his observations at the time of a land survey, or land reallotment, or when the number of people in the family becomes excessive. But when revising the tags there must be no mistake in the matter of recording *"myōzu"* or *"nago,"* and a check shall be made with the old register. If the branch family was established after the last tag inspection, the record shall be made according to the statement of the agricultural magistrate.

7. When a peasant, with the permission of the agricultural mag-

istrate, relinquishes his position as *myōzu* to his adopted heir or to his natural heir, he shall have the *myōzu* [designation] corrected at the time of tag inspection on the basis of verifying documents written by the agricultural promoter and the *shōya*. If he is relinquishing his position to someone other than his adopted heir or natural heir, he must report to the agricultural office, and the *myōzu* position shall be determined on the basis of written testimony of the agricultural magistrate.

Proviso: Application for the departure or addition of *nago* in the household shall be made at the agricultural office, and it shall be determined on the basis of written testimony of the agricultural magistrate.

8. Anyone who attaches his land allotment shall record on his tag and in the register that the previous *myōzu* was so-and-so and the present *myōzu* is so-and-so, and the recipient of the land shall record on his tag and in the register that the present *myōzu* is so-and-so and the previous *myōzu* was so-and-so.

Proviso: When a peasant gives his son a name consisting of one character only, male and female [names] become indistinguishable. Therefore, such names shall not be given.

9. Among peasants, those who enter a side notation that they are chronically ill or physically handicapped shall be issued a tag after they are personally examined. If a person has entered an incorrect side notation, he shall be reported without fail.

10. Daughters and female and male servants of shrine and temple-gate personnel are permitted to marry into households of peasants and fishermen, but those who do so shall correct their tags to those of peasants and fishermen.

Proviso: Inasmuch as the above type marriages are permitted, if the wife's tag is not corrected in such instances, it would appear that she is employed as a day laborer in lieu of payment of interest on a loan. Thus, both parties shall be fined one *kammon* each. Children born of such a union shall be issued a tag at the peasant or fishing village. Even though they appeal that there was nothing wrong with their marriage, their appeal shall be denied.

11. No peasant or shrine personnel members shall presume to assign himself a title of office.

12. Although male and female peasants are prohibited from

leaving [their district], they are permitted to leave for a fixed term of service with a Kagoshima samurai if he has a verifying statement from the agricultural magistrate. However, this shall not be interpreted as a change of registry.

13. For marriages and adoptions of peasants and of rural townsmen, tags shall be corrected with verifying statements written by the *shōya*, the *bettō*, and the agricultural promoter.

Proviso: When a person leaves for another district for marriage or adoption, his name shall be removed from the register on the basis of a permit written by the *gōshi toshiyori* if his departure is from a district, and by the *yakunin* if the departure is from a private domain. One may come from a rural town to enter a peasant household by marriage or adoption, but it is prohibited to leave a peasant village for a rural town, nor can people in rural towns have reciprocity for marriages and adoptions with families in towns and fishing villages.

14. When people from other places enter a farm village or rural town by marriage or adoption or for other reasons and later return to their original homes because of divorce or for other particulars, a permit written by the agricultural magistrate is required.

Proviso: If a child is born [to the above people], a tag on the father's side shall be requested on the basis of a verifying statement by the agricultural magistrate.

15. While it is permitted for a person from a rural town to marry into a peasant household, she shall obtain a wife's tag. Moreover, if a peasant obtains a bride, but does not correct her tag to that of "peasant wife," it would appear that he is employing her as a day laborer in lieu of interest payment on a debt. Thus both parties shall be fined one *kammon* each. Though they may report that there was nothing wrong with their marriage, their appeal shall be denied.

16. *Gōshi* and peasants, who, due to an offense, are placed in custody of a private domain with the status of servant, shall all receive their tags at the place of custody, as ordered in the fourth month, second year of Kōka (1845).

17. The rural town of Yokoi, being a regular stopping and resting point for the daimyo on his [*sankin kōtai*] trips to and from Edo, should be well provided to lodge the lord and his retinue. However

the town is so impoverished that the residents are unable to seek wives. Therefore the rural town of Yokoi shall have marriage reciprocity with agricultural villages, and these marriages shall take place with the written permission of the agricultural magistrate.

18. Residents of the rural towns of Takaoka, Aya, Mukasa, and Kuraoka are permitted to have marriage reciprocity with peasants. These marriages shall take place with the written permission of the agricultural magistrate. Marriages by those who do not have such permits, or marriages with peasants in the interior area [neighboring Kagoshima city], are strictly forbidden. In these four districts daughters of servants of *gōshi* shall be permitted marriages with residents of these towns, but daughters of these rural townsmen are prohibited from going to [the families of] *gōshi* servants.

19. Among the rural townsmen of the districts of Takaoka, Aya, Kuraoka, and Mukasa, the *myōzu* and their relatives including their children, uncles, nephews, and cousins, are permitted the use of surnames.

20. Residents of the rural town of Yoshida in Morokata county, upon petition, shall be permitted marriages with daughters of peasants.

Proviso: A permit from the agricultural magistrate shall be required as in the past.

21. Among the rural townsmen of the districts of Iino and Kakutō and in Itsukamachi and Tōkamachi of Kobayashi district, only the *myōzu* are permitted the use of surnames.

22. Residents of the rural town of Nojiri district, being assigned to the Kamiya guard post, are called to service by the guard station whenever there are criminals in the area. In recent years, due to poverty, they have been unable to arrange marriages appropriate to their position, and gradually the number of townsmen has been decreasing so that service to the daimyo will undoubtedly be hindered. Therefore, upon petition, they shall be permitted marriages with daughters of peasants in the districts of Nojiri and Kobayashi. However, this shall not be construed as a precedent.

23. The rural town of Yoshimatsu district has served as the lodging place for couriers on the Kuma road, and in addition, it has been the lodging place for officials on their way toward [the

region of] Masaki. But in recent years the town has gradually become impoverished, so that of the original sixteen households there are now only eight. The men are all single, so that the town will be unable to survive, and gradually it will become difficult to perform the services for the daimyo. Therefore, upon petition, these townsmen shall be granted marriage reciprocity with peasants.

24. Residents of the rural town of Ōkuchi district, having been poor for a succession of years, were unable to bring in people for marriage from rural towns of other districts, and the men were all without wives. In recent years their population decreased, and it became difficult for them to fulfill their public services. If this situation continued eventually the town would be unable to survive. Therefore they petitioned for permission to bring in peasants for marriages. Because of the difficulty in rendering public services, and especially because of the town's location, which borders on another domain, permission was granted as petitioned in the fourth year of Hōreki (1754).

25. Because the residents of the rural town of Takasaki district were few and particularly poor, there was no influx of people from other districts for marriages. Upon petition, in the fifth year of Hōreki (1755) permission for marriages with peasants was granted. Moreover, again upon petition, permission was granted for marriages with female servants of *gōshi* in the district, as ordered in the fourth month, ninth year of Tempō (1838).

26. Residents of the rural town of Takaono district have been in extreme poverty for many years past. As they carried out corvée labor services the same as peasants, and because the town had difficulty surviving, their petition for marriages with peasants was granted in the seventh year of Hōreki (1757).

27. Residents of the rural town of Yamano district, being impoverished, were unable to travel far to other districts to arrange for marriages. Upon petition, permission was granted in the eighth year of Hōreki (1758) for marriage reciprocity with peasants and for incoming marriages with *hitokerai* and servants.

28. Residents of the rural town of Kurino district, being poor, were unable to go to other areas to arrange marriages. Upon petition, they were granted permission in the eighth year of Hōreki (1758) for marriage reciprocity with peasants within the district.

29. Residents of the rural town of Tsuruda district, though generally poor, in recent years became increasingly impoverished, and they had no one to render public labor service. Upon their petition, in the ninth year of Hōreki (1759) they were granted permission to marry peasants in the entire district.

Proviso: While permission was granted as stated above, upon another petition, permission was granted for marriage reciprocity with peasants in neighboring districts for a period of ten years from the seventh year of Bunsei (1824) to the fourth year of Tempō (1833). This period expired, and upon further petition, permission was granted for marriage reciprocity with peasants within their own district and in the districts of Sashi, Miyanojō, and Ōmura for ten years beginning with the ninth year of Tempō (1838), but the period expired by the fourth year of Kōka (1847).

30. Residents of the rural town of Odori district, having become poor, were unable to arrange marriages appropriate to their station. Upon their petition, they were granted permission for a limited period to have marriage reciprocity with peasants within their own district and in neighboring districts after the eleventh year of Hōreki (1761). The period having expired, again permission was granted for marriage reciprocity with peasants within their district and in neighboring districts for a period of twenty years beginning with the eighth year of Tempō (1837).

31. People from other domains who have received permanent residency tags and are settled in rural towns shall have verifying statements written by the *shōya* or *bettō* and the agricultural promoter whenever they enter or depart for marriage with residents of rural towns or with peasants of the several districts.

32. Peasants on *ukimen* land and peasants who have transferred must have a verifying statement written by the agricultural magistrate.

33. As for additions or removals of tag [registration] for men and women from other domains who were assigned in previous years to peasants, a written statement by the agricultural magistrate shall be required.

Proviso: A verifying statement from the office of term employment shall not be required.

34. When male and female servants of peasants leave for em-

ployment with a peasant in another district, the transfer from the place of tag registration shall require written statements by the *gōshi toshiyori* and agricultural promoter of both districts. Furthermore, when the transfer is to an area within the same district, the transfer of the place of tag registration shall require only the written statements of the agricultural promoter and the *shōya*.

35. When a female servant of a peasant marries a peasant, she shall have her tag corrected to that of "peasant's wife" at the time of tag inspection with verifying statements written by the agricultural promoter and the *shōya*.

36. Because residents of rural towns and fishing villages of the various districts are of the same status as peasants and fishermen, they shall not be permitted the use of surnames. However, among those residing in the *han's* border districts, the *myōzu* alone, upon their petition, shall be permitted the use of surnames.

37. Residents of the two rural towns of Itsukamachi and Tōkamachi in Kobayashi district, being poor, were unable to arrange marriages appropriate to their station, and the men were all without wives. Upon their request for permission to bring in by marriage daughters of shrine personnel, temple-gate personnel, and peasants who reside not only in Kobayashi district but also in the neighboring districts, the petition was granted for the succeeding fifteen years as ordered in the third month, twelfth year of Bunka (1815). However, the period having expired, again upon their petition, permission was granted as before for fifteen years beginning with the thirteenth year of Bunsei (1830). When the period expired, once more permission was granted as before for fifteen years beginning with the second year of Kōka (1845).

38. Residents of the rural town in Soki district, being few in number, were unable to arrange marriages appropriate to their station. Upon their petition, permission for marriage reciprocity with peasants was granted twice since the twelfth year of Bunka (1815), each time for ten-year periods. However, the period expired, and permission was granted as before for [another] ten years beginning with the second year of Kōka (1845).

39. Residents of the rural town of Ei district, being poor, were unable to arrange marriages appropriate to their station. Upon their request, since the twelfth year of Bunka (1815) permission

was granted from time to time for fixed periods for marriage reciprocity with fishermen and peasants within their own district as
well as in the districts of Chiran, Kago, Kawanabe, Yamada in
the county of Kawanabe, Kiire, Imaizumi, Ibusuki, and Yamagawa. These periods having expired, again permission was granted
as in the past for twenty years beginning with the eighth year of
Tempō (1837).

40. Residents of the rural town in Yamada district in Aira
county, being poor, were unable to arrange marriages appropriate
to their station. Upon their petition, since the twelfth year of
Bunka (1815) for a fixed period, they were granted permission for
marriage reciprocity with peasants as well as with servants of *gōshi*
within their district [of Yamada] and with peasants in the districts of Mizobe, Kajiki, Chōsa, and Shigetomi. The period expired, and again permission was granted as in the past for ten years
beginning with the eighth year of Tempō (1837), but this period
expired in the third year of Kōka (1846).

41. Residents of the rural town in Ōsaki district, being poor,
were unable to arrange marriages appropriate to their station.
Upon their request, since the fourth year of Meiwa (1767) they
were granted permission to bring in by marriage peasants from the
districts of Ōsaki and Shibushi. Again, upon petition, they were
permitted marriage reciprocity with peasants of Kushira district
for ten years beginning with the seventh year of Bunsei (1824).
However, the period expired and a renewal of permission was announced as in the past for another ten years beginning with the
eighth year of Tempō (1837), but this period expired in the third
year of Kōka (1846).

42. Residents of the rural town of Jōnomachi in Ichiki district,
being impoverished, were unable to have marriage reciprocity.
Upon their request, permission was granted since the fourth year of
Meiwa (1767) to bring in by marriage peasants in the district of
Ichiki. Again upon their request, they were granted permission
for marriage reciprocity with peasants of the districts of Kushikino,
Ijūin, Hioki, Yoshitoshi, Nagayoshi, Izaku, Tabuse, and Ata, for
ten years beginning with the ninth year of Tempō (1838), but this
period expired in the fourth year of Kōka (1847).

43. Residents of the rural town in Nojiri district, being impover-

ished, upon their petition, were granted permission for marriages with peasants within their own district and in the districts of Takasaki, Takahara, and Kobayashi in the fifth year of Meiwa (1768).

44. Residents of the rural town in Kushira district, being impoverished, upon their petition, were granted permission for twenty years beginning with the sixth year of Meiwa (1769) to bring in by marriage peasants within their own district and in the districts of Kōyama and Ōsaki. However, the period expired in the eighth year of Temmei (1788), after which [such marriages] were not permitted. Again upon their petition, permission was renewed twice for twenty years each, beginning with the fifth year of Kansei (1793). When these periods expired, a further renewal was granted as in the past for twenty years beginning with the fifth year of Tempō (1834).

45. Residents of the rural town in Kōyama district, being poor, upon their petition, from time to time were permitted for fixed periods, beginning with the seventh year of Meiwa (1770), to bring in by marriage peasants from within their own district and fishing villagers of Hamiura. These periods having expired, permission was granted again repeatedly, beginning with the twelfth year of Kansei (1800), for marriage reciprocity with the fishing village of Tōjinmachi in Kushira district and with the fishing village of Hami. These periods expired, and permission was granted again in the second month, fourth year of Kaei (1851), as in the past, for twenty years, the period to begin in the following year.

46. Residents of the rural town in Hazuki district, being in financial straits, were unable to arrange marriages appropriate to their station. Upon their request, permission was granted for twenty years beginning with the seventh year of Meiwa (1770) to bring in by marriage peasants within their own district and from the districts of Yamano, Ōguchi, and Soki. However, the period expired by the ninth year of Temmei (1789), and again upon petition, permission was granted for twenty years beginning with the eleventh year of Kansei (1799) to bring in by marriage peasants within their own district and from the four neighboring districts of Yamano, Ōguchi, Magoshi, and Soki. This period expired in the fifteenth year of Bunsei (1830) [sic, Bunka 1818?], and again

upon petition, permission was granted in the sixth year of Bunsei (1823) for the following twenty years to bring in by marriage peasants from within their own district and from the districts of Yamano, Ōguchi, Magoshi, Honjō, and Soki. This period expired by the thirteenth year of Tempo (1842), and once again permission was granted to bring in by marriage peasants of Hishikari region [Ōguchi, Yamano, Soki, Hazuki, and Magoshi] for twenty years beginning with the first year of Kaei (1848).

47. The two villages of Minamimatamura and Kitamatamura in Yatsushiro in Takaoka district had too few women and too many single men. In such a situation there were not even enough cultivators. Consequently, upon their petition, from the seventh year of Meiwa (1770) they were granted permission to bring in by marriage daughters of peasants from the lord's domain of Sadohara. A petition shall be submitted at that time and care shall be taken to avoid errors in such matters as the statement of religious affiliation.

48. The village of Fukatoshi in Takaoka district, having few women, petitioned as above, and in the tenth month, eighth year of Kansei (1796) permission was granted to bring in by marriage daughters of peasants residing in the lord's domain of Sadohara. Of course, a petition shall be submitted on such occasions, and care shall be taken to avoid errors in such matters as the statement of religious affiliation.

49. Residents of the rural town in Sueyoshi district, being poor, did not have people from other districts coming in by marriage. Upon their petition, they were granted permission for marriage reciprocity with peasants within their district as of the third month, fourth year of Meiwa (1767).

50. Residents of the rural town in Imaizumi district, being poor, were unable to arrange marriages appropriate to their station. Since the second year of Meiwa (1765) repeatedly they were granted marriage reciprocity for fixed periods of time, certainly with peasants and fishing villagers residing within their own district, but also with those in neighboring districts. These periods expired, and again they were granted marriage reciprocity with peasants and fishing villagers residing within their own district and in the districts of Kiire, Ibusuki, and Ei for a period of ten

years beginning with the eighth year of Tempō (1837). The period expired, and upon further petition, permission was granted for marriage reciprocity with peasants, fishing villagers, and rural townsmen residing in the districts of Kiire, Ibusuki, Ei, Taniyama, Yamagawa, Chiran, Kago, and Bōdomari for the following twenty years beginning with the fourth year of Kōka (1847).

51. Residents of the rural town in Tsuneyoshi district, being poor, were unable to arrange marriages appropriate to their station, and gradually their population decreased. Thus upon their petition, since the ninth month, fourth year of Meiwa (1767) they were granted permission to marry daughters of peasants within their district.

52. Residents of the rural town in Matsuyama district became impoverished, so upon their petition permission was granted repeatedly since the ninth year of Meiwa (1772), each time for fifteen years, to have marriage reciprocity with peasants within the district. The periods expired, and upon further petition permission was extended in the eighth year of Tempō (1837), as in the past, for fifteen years.

53. Residents of the rural town in Ōmura district, being poor, were unable to arrange marriages appropriate to their station. Upon their petition, permission was granted repeatedly for marriage reciprocity with peasants within their own district and in neighboring districts for definite periods beginning with the ninth year of Meiwa (1772). These periods having expired, permission was granted for marriage reciprocity with peasants residing in the districts of Miyanojō, Sashi, and Yamazaki for ten years beginning with the eighth year of Bunsei (1825). However, this period expired, and again permission was granted for marriage reciprocity with peasants within their district and in the districts of Miyanojō, Yamazaki, Imuta, Sashi, and Kuroki for ten years beginning with the ninth year of Tempō (1838). The period having expired again, permission was granted as in the past for another ten years beginning with the fourth year of Kaei (1851).

54. Residents of the rural town in Ijūin district, being poor, were unable to arrange marriages appropriate to their station. Upon their petition, they were granted permission for marriage reciprocity with peasants residing within their own district for a

period of ten years beginning with the fifth month, ninth year of Meiwa (1772). However, this period expired, and upon their petition, they were granted permission for marriage reciprocity with peasants in their own district and in neighboring districts since the fifth year of Temmei (1785).

55. Residents of the rural town in Mizobe district, being poor, were unable to arrange marriages appropriate to their station. Upon their request, they were granted permission for marriage reciprocity with peasants residing within their own district for fifteen years beginning with the fifth month, ninth year of Meiwa (1772). However, the period expired, and upon further petitions, permission was granted repeatedly for marriage reciprocity with peasants residing in their own district and in the districts of Yamada in Aira county, Kajiki, Hinatayama, and Yokogawa each for periods of ten years beginning with the sixth year of Temmei (1786). However, these periods expired, and permission again was granted as in the past for ten years beginning with the eighth year of Tempō (1837). The period expired in the third year of Kōka (1846).

56. Peasants in Ushine district, being poor, were unable to arrange marriages appropriate to their station. Upon their petition repeatedly they were granted permission for marriage reciprocity between peasants and fishing villagers residing within the district for definite periods beginning with the fifth month, ninth year of Meiwa (1772). These periods expired, and upon further petition, permission was granted as in the past for fifteen years beginning with the third year of Tempō (1832).

57. Residents of the rural town in Yoshida district of Kagoshima county, having become impoverished, upon their petition, repeatedly were granted permission for marriage reciprocity with peasants within their own district and in other districts for definite periods beginning with the thirteenth year of Hōreki (1763). These periods expired, and upon further petition, permission was granted as in the past for twenty years beginning with the eighth year of Tempō (1837).

58. Residents of the rural town in Takarabe district, upon their petition, were granted permission in the first year of Meiwa (1764)

to bring in by marriage peasants residing in the districts of Miyakonojō, Sueyoshi, and Fukuyama.

59. Manjirō and the late Kamejirō of the rural town in Takarabe district, in view of the daimyo's situation at the time, petitioned their desire to present him with over six thousand cryptomeria stands from their *buichiyama* forest land located in Kitamatamura of the same district. It was ordered as petitioned. These two men and their late father have often given aid to those in extreme need, and on such occasions they were rewarded with gifts from the *han* lord. In addition, in the year of the dragon (1808?), when the lord called for contributions for the *han* debt, they each presented funds of 150 *kammon*, for which act they were each granted an exemption for ten years from any public labor obligation. Now at this time, as stated above, they have petitioned their desire to present cryptomeria trees from their *buichiyama* forest land. As they are particularly praiseworthy for their spirit, by the lord's special consideration, both men for their lifetime shall be granted the use of surnames and the right to wear short swords, as ordered in the third month, ninth year of Bunka (1812).

60. The families of those serving as *toshigyōji* and *otona* in the two rural towns in Kokubu district shall be permitted the use of surnames, as ordered in the first month, fifth year of Temmei (1785).

61. In special consideration of their background, even those in the main rural town of Tōjinmachi in Kokubu district who hold residential land, including those who establish branch families, shall be permitted to become *myōzu* with the use of surnames. Those who have sold their residential land shall be deprived of their surnames as ordered in the sixth month, seventh year of Bunsei (1824).

62. In the town of Komuramachi in Kokubu district, upon their petition and in consideration of their good lineage, permission is granted for the use of surnames to *toshigyōji* who have retired after faithfully fulfilling their duties and to heads of *myōzu* households, as ordered in the fifth month, third year of Bunsei (1830).

63. Residents of the rural town in Takahara district, being

small in number, were unable to arrange marriages appropriate to their station. Upon their petition, they were granted permission to marry peasants in Takahara district during a period of twenty years beginning with the tenth year of An'ei (1781). Since the period expired this year (1800), upon petition, permission was granted to bring in by marriage peasants and temple-gate personnel within their district and from neighboring districts for twenty years from 1801, as ordered in the third month, twelfth year of Kansei (1800). When this latter period expired in the third year of Bunsei (1820), again upon further petition, permission was granted as in the past for twenty years beginning with the seventh year of Bunsei (1824). This period having expired in the fourteenth year of Tempō (1843), again upon further petition, permission was granted for twenty years beginning with the third year of Kōka (1846) for marriage reciprocity with shrine personnel, temple-gate personnel, and peasants within their own district and in neighboring districts.

64. Residents of the rural town in Suki district, being small in number, were unable to arrange marriages on a reciprocal basis. Upon their petition, beginning with the first month, eighth year of An'ei (1779), they were repeatedly granted permission for twenty years each time to bring in by marriage peasants who resided in their own district. These periods expired, and the order was renewed as in the past for twenty years beginning with the eighth year of Tempō (1837).

65. As the district of Takajō in Morokata county is located on the border with other domains, residents of its rural town diligently practice *jūjitsu* and the art of capturing criminals and the like. When criminals are apprehended in other districts and brought in for the night for lodging, the residents are ordered to stand guard or are assigned to such tasks as refastening the bonds of the prisoners. Moreover, when they are called upon to cross over into neighboring domains in connection with official work such as gathering information, it is always inconvenient for them to be without surnames. There being pleas from the district inspectors to this effect, in the fifth year of Temmei (1785), in accordance with the petition, permission was granted to allow those down to the *myōzu* status the right to use surnames.

66. Because there were few residents in the rural town in Yunoo, they had difficulty arranging marriages on a reciprocal basis. Upon their petition, permission was repeatedly granted since the seventh year of An'ei (1778) for periods of twenty years to bring in by marriage peasants within their own district and from neighboring districts. These periods expired, and upon further petition, permission was granted again as in the past for twenty years as of the second year of Kōka (1845).

67. Residents of the rural town in Kamō district, being poor, had difficulty arranging marriages on a basis of reciprocity. Upon their petition, permission was granted for a period of fifteen years beginning with the seventh month, second year of Temmei (1782), for marriage reciprocity with servants of *gōshi* in the district and with the peasants in the same district. The period having expired, it was announced in the eleventh month, thirteenth year of Bunsei (1830), that upon petition permission was now being granted once more for fifteen years, as it had been repeatedly in the past. However, this period expired by the first year of Kōka (1844), and upon further petition permission was granted again as in the past for fifteen years beginning with the third year of Kōka (1846).

68. Residents of the two rural towns in Kokubu district found it difficult to have marriage reciprocity only among themselves. Upon petition, they were granted permission repeatedly since the sixth year of Temmei (1786), each time for ten years, to marry townspeople, fishing villagers, temple-gate personnel, and peasants. These periods having expired, again upon petition, they were granted permission for ten years beginning with the fourth year of Kōka (1847) for marriage reciprocity with townspeople, fishing villagers, temple-gate personnel, servants of *gōshi*, and peasants who resided not only in their own district, but also in the three town districts in Kagoshima [city] and in the [administrative] districts of Shigetomi, Chōsa, Kajiki, Shikine, Fukuyama, Ushine, Tarumizu, Shibushi, Kiyomizu, Soōnokōri, Hinatayama, Yokogawa, Miyakonojō, and Takarabe.

69. Upon their petitions, the use of surnames was granted in the seventh month, sixth year of Temmei (1786) to the following twenty-eight persons who are residents in the rural town in the district of Sueyoshi: Iwasaki Niuemon, Katō Teiuemon, Oka-

zaki Den'uemon, Hashiguchi Jisuke, Katō Jisuke, Hashiguchi Zembei, Hashiguchi Den'uemon, Katō Gorōuemon, Katō Yotarō, Katō Jirōbei, Katō Den'uemon, Okazaki Heijirō, Miyata Tauemon, widow [with son of minor age] of Okazaki Heisuke, Iwasaki Nisuke, widow [with son of minor age] of Hashiguchi Zensuke, Iwasaki Riuemon, Katō Denshirō, Miyata Kihei, Hashiguchi Zenzaemon, Inomata Zensuke, Katō Mansuke, Iwasaki Zenroku, Miyata Takichi, Iwasaki Genzaemon, Iwasaki Nitarō, Hashiguchi Kotarō, and Hashiguchi Kanetarō.

70. The following three persons of the rural town in Sueyoshi district, Iwasaki Gentarō, Katō Man'uemon, and Iwasaki Uemon, upon their petition, have been granted the use of surnames, as of the fifth month, twelfth year of Kansei (1800).

71. Residents of the rural town in Kawanabe district, upon their petition, were granted permission for marriage reciprocity with peasants within their own district and in the districts of Yamada in Kawanabe county, Chiran, and Ata for twenty years beginning with the seventh month, fifth year of An'ei (1776). The period expired in the seventh month, eighth year of Kansei (1796) and was not renewed thereafter. However, upon further petitions, permission was granted twice since the third month, eleventh year of Kansei (1799), for twenty-year periods, for marriage reciprocity with peasants in their own district and in the districts of Ata, Kaseda, Chiran, and Yamada in Kawanabe county. These periods having expired, upon further petition, permission was granted for twenty years beginning with the tenth year of Tempō (1839), for marriage reciprocity with peasants, fishermen, servants, and temple-gate personnel residing in their own district and in the districts of Ata, Kaseda, Ei, Yamada of Kawanabe county, and Taniyama.

72. Because there were few households and few people in the rural town of Furueura in Hanaoka district, the residents had difficulty maintaining marriage reciprocity. Thus in the second month, second year of Bunka (1805), upon petition, permission was granted to rural townsmen for marriage reciprocity with fishermen, and peasants within their own district. This period having expired, again upon petition, permission was granted to the rural townsmen for ten years beginning with the eighth year of Bunsei

(1825) for marriage reciprocity with fishing villagers, and peasants within their own district and with those residing in the neighboring districts of Tarumizu, Shinjō, Kanoya, and Ōaira. The period having expired, further permission was granted as in the past for ten years beginning with the sixth year of Tempō (1835), but this period expired in the first year of Kōka (1844).

73. Residents of the rural town in Yamazaki district, being generally poor, had difficulty arranging marriages appropriate to their station. Since the twelfth year of Bunka (1815) they have been granted permission from time to time for specified periods to bring in by marriage members of shrine personnel, temple-gate personnel, and peasant families residing not only in their own district but also in neighboring districts. These periods having expired, further permission was granted as in the past for ten years beginning with the fourth year of Kōka (1847).

74. Residents of the rural town in Taki district in Taki county, being poor, had difficulty arranging marriages appropriate to their station. Upon their petition they were repeatedly granted permission since the twelfth year of Kansei (1800), each time for ten years, for marriage reciprocity with peasants. These periods having expired, again, as in the past, permission was granted for ten years beginning with the eighth year of Tempō (1837). However, the period expired in the third year of Kōka (1846).

75. Residents of the rural town in Chiran district, being poor, upon their request repeatedly were granted permission since the second month, twelfth year of Kansei (1800), each time for ten years, for marriage reciprocity with peasants residing in their own district and in the neighboring districts of Kiire, Ei, Kago, Yamada of Kawanabe county, and Kawanabe. These periods having expired, upon petition further permission was granted as in the past for ten years beginning with the eighth year of Tempō (1837). However, this period expired in the third year of Kōka (1846).

76. Residents of the rural town in Yokogawa district, being impoverished, were unable to arrange marriages suitable to their station. Thus, they have been granted permission repeatedly since the third month, twelfth year of Kansei (1800), for specified periods, for marriage reciprocity with peasants residing not only in their own district but also in neighboring districts and with

people [from other domains] who work in the Yamagano gold mines and who register as residents of the *han*. These periods expired in the tenth year of Tempō (1839).

77. Residents of the rural town in Hiwaki district, being poor, were granted permission in the twelfth year of Bunka (1815) for a specified period, for marriage reciprocity with peasants in their own district and in the districts of Iriki, Yamazaki and Tōgō. This period having expired, further permission was granted as in the past for a period of ten years beginning with the eighth year of Tempō (1837), but this period expired in the third year of Kōka (1846).

78. Residents of the rural town in Maganda district, being reduced in number, were unable to arrange marriages appropriate to their station. They were therefore granted permission in the sixth year of Bunsei (1823), for a period of ten years thereafter, for marriage reciprocity with peasants residing in their district. This period expired in the third year of Tempō (1832), and upon further petition, permission was granted as in the past for ten years beginning with the ninth year of Tempō (1838). This period expired in the fourth year of Kōka (1847).

79. Residents of the rural town in Noda district, being poor, upon petition, were granted permission in the seventh year of Bunsei (1824), for a period of ten years thereafter, for marriage reciprocity with peasants residing within their district. But this period expired in the fourth year of Tempō (1833).

80. Because the residents of the Fumotomachi in the district of Izumi were impoverished, few people were brought in by marriage from the rural towns of other districts, and the men were all without wives. Upon their petition, it was announced in the ninth month, eighth year of Bunsei (1825) that for a time they shall be permitted marriages with both male and female residents of the town in Akune district, Ōshōjimachi in Mizuhiki district, and Mukōdamachi in Kumanojō district.

81. Residents of the rural town in Kanoya district, being impoverished, were unable to arrange marriages appropriate to their station. Upon their petition, they were granted permission for ten years beginning with the ninth year of Tempō (1838) for marriage reciprocity not only with fishing villagers and peasants

residing in their own district but also with townspeople in the three townships of Kagoshima and with peasants and fishing villagers in the districts of Takakuma, Kushira, Kōyama, Aira, Ōaira, Ōnejime, Hanaoka, Shinjō, and Tarumizu. However, this period expired in the fourth year of Kōka (1847).

82. Residents of the rural town of Aira district, being poor, were unable to arrange marriages appropriate to their station. Upon their petition, therefore, they were granted permission in the first year of Kaei (1848) for a period of twenty years thereafter for marriage and adoptive reciprocity with fishing villagers and rural townsmen in the districts of Kōyama, Kushira, Uchinoura, Ōsaki, Shibushi, Kanoya, Hanaoka, Shinjō, and Tarumizu.

83. Residents of the rural town in Tōgō district, being poor, were unable to arrange marriages appropriate to their station. Upon their petition, permission was granted for ten years beginning with the second year of Kōka (1845) for marriage reciprocity among peasants, fishing villagers and rural townsmen residing within the district.

XVI. Regulations on the inspection of tags of fishing villagers and of those attached to the office of maritime magistracy

1. Residents of the fishing village of Matsubaraura and the peasant village of Shioyazai, which are private possessions of Shimazu Sazen located in Chōsa district, became impoverished; in addition, the fishing village of Wakimotoura was made a part of Shigetomi district. Because the result was an increase in corvée obligations, and as the gradual decrease in population made the fulfillment of these obligations difficult, marriage reciprocity was permitted for a fixed period of time between the fishing village and the peasant village. The period expired, and upon further petition, permission was granted as in the past for twenty years beginning with the seventh year of Temmei (1787). This period expired, and again upon petition, permission was granted as in the past for twenty years beginning with the fifth year of Bunka (1808). Upon the expiration of this term and upon further petition, as in the past another twenty-year period was granted as of the second month, second year of Tempō (1831). This period expired in the third year of Kaei (1850).

2. Regular ship captains attached to the two offices of maritime magistrates shall record their ages and their surnames on their tags and in the register. Moreover, regular boatmen and those of lower status who have not had surnames but who have been wearing swords shall have surnames henceforth, as ordered in the fifth month, eighth year of Bunsei (1825).

3. Retainers of castle-town samurai and shrine and temple-gate personnel are permitted to be taken in by marriage by fishing villagers, but if children are born by their secret liaisons with fishing villagers, the children shall be issued tags of the fishing villagers. To have such secret relations is an offense against the *han* law, so both parties shall pay a fine of one *kammon* each.

Proviso: If the daughter or maid servant of a fishing villager has a temporary relationship with a servant of a castle-town samurai, *hitokerai*, or a member of shrine or temple-gate personnel and a child is born, the child shall be issued tags of the fishing villager. Fines shall be levied as stipulated above.

4. Male and female servants of castle-town samurai and male and female servants of *hitokerai*, shrine personnel, and temple-gate personnel may enter by marriage or adoption into families of fishing villagers, but the facts for such marriage or adoption shall be ascertained by supporting statements written by the master and the supervisory chief. Those who are found to be of good character shall be issued a tag at the fishing village by the village functionary. It shall not be necessary to report to the maritime magistrate.

Proviso: If the woman's tag is not corrected to that of "wife" tag despite the fact that marriage is permitted as above, and she continues work as a servant, it would appear that she is kept as a day laborer to pay the interest on a debt. In such cases a fine of one *kammon* each shall be levied on both parties. If she gives birth to a child, the child shall be issued a tag of the fishing villager. Even though they may appeal that there was nothing wrong with the marriage, the appeal shall be rejected.

5. When a person who is attached to the office of maritime service leaves for another [jurisdictional] area, a written statement by the maritime magistrate is required. Entries into and departures from [households] on a basis of reciprocity [for marriages and adoptions] among people assigned to the office of maritime service shall require the written statement of the ship captain.

6. Departures from or entries into [households] by marriage of residents of fishing villages with residents of other fishing villages shall require the written statement of the maritime magistrate.

7. Marriages among any of the fishing villagers within the

same district shall require only the written statement of the fishing village [*gōshi*] functionary.

8. A fishing villager who yields his *myōzu* position and his surname, as well as one who wishes to establish a branch family, shall report to the office of maritime service and the maritime magistrate shall carefully study the matter on the basis of supporting documents.

9. When either a male or female child of a fishing villager is made a foster child of another fishing villager, or if a wife has brought along a child [to her new family], the matter shall be reported to the office of maritime service and the decision to register the child as foster child shall be investigated by the maritime magistrate on the basis of supporting documents.

10. While it is not necessary to report to the office of maritime service a tag change for a maid servant of a fishing villager to that of "wife of fishing village resident," the change to "wife" tag shall be made on the basis of a written statement by the fishing village functionary.

11. When a male or female servant of a fishing villager departs for Kagoshima or for some other district, there shall be a report from that district to the office of maritime service, and the withdrawal from the place of tag registration shall be accomplished on the basis of a written statement by the maritime magistrate. If the person is withdrawing [from his household to another household] within the same fishing village, it shall not be necessary to report to the office of maritime service. The withdrawal from the household of tag registration shall be accomplished on the basis of a written statement by the fishing village functionary.

12. Because of the good lineage of the family with the surname of Yotsumoto in the fishing village of Matsuzakimachi in Taniyama district, upon their petition, they were permitted to record their surname both on their tags and in the register.

13. The three fishing villages of Matsuzakimachi, Hirakawaura, and Wadahama in Taniyama district, being generally poor, have had a decline in population in recent years, and their residents were not able to arrange marriages appropriate to their station. Upon their petition, therefore, for a period of ten years

beginning with the fifteenth year of Tempō (1844) they were granted marriage reciprocity with peasants, attendants, and servants residing within their own district and in neighboring districts.

14. As for *ura machi* ["town by the inlet"] and *hama machi* ["town by the beach"], since the people residing in *ura* and *hama* are of the same status, at the time of tag inspection, *ura* and *hama* shall be treated alike.

15. Those assigned to the office of maritime service shall be permitted marriage reciprocity with residents of the three districts of Kamimachi, Shimomachi, and Nishidamachi [in Kagoshima city].

16. Fishing villagers and townsmen, who enter a side notation that they are chronically ill or disabled, shall be issued a tag after they are personally examined. If there should be any discrepancy in the side notation this shall be reported without fail.

17. Because the fishing village of Tōjinmachi in Kushira district became especially impoverished and her population gradually diminished, no one came into the village for marriage. Upon their petition, therefore, they were granted permission in the tenth year of Hōreki (1760) to bring in by marriage people from the rural town in Kushira district.

18. The residents of the fishing village of Tōjinmachi in Kushira district were granted permission to marry as provided in the above article, but, upon their petition, beginning with the eighth year of Kansei (1796) they were granted marriage reciprocity with rural townspeople in neighboring districts as well as with peasants within their own district for ten-year periods in each case. These periods expired, and permission was granted again as in the past for ten years beginning with the seventh year of Tempō (1836). This period expired in the second year of Kōka (1845).

19. Residents of the fishing villages of Kitatakasuura and Minamitakasuura in Kanoya district, being poor, were unable to arrange marriages with their equals in other fishing villages. As a result many men were without wives. Therefore, marriage reciprocity was permitted for ten years with peasants residing in their own district and in the closest districts, with people in Shinhama, and

with residents of the rural town of Kanoya district, as ordered in the second month, second year of Tempō (1831). However, this period expired, and upon further petition, permission was granted as in the past for a period of ten years beginning with the twelfth year of Tempō (1841), and this expired in the third year of Kaei (1850).

20. The fishing villagers in Tarumizu district, being economically pressed, were unable to arrange marriages with other fishing villages. Upon their petition, therefore, from time to time they were granted permission for marriage reciprocity with the peasants residing in their own district for periods of twenty years each, beginning with the sixth year of Meiwa (1769). These periods expired, and upon further petition, permission was extended as in the past for twenty years beginning with the fifth year of Tempō (1834).

21. As for the fishing village of Kunukibaru in Tarumizu district, in various documents it is recorded as Kunukibaru*ura*, while on the tags it has been recorded as Kunukibaru*hama*. However, henceforth both on tags and in the documents it shall be recorded as Kunukibaru*ura*, as ordered in the intercalary ninth month, fourteenth year of Tempō (1843).

22. Fishing villagers in the district of Kiire, being impoverished, upon their petition, were granted marriage reciprocity with peasants residing within their own district repeatedly for twenty years each time, beginning with the ninth year of Meiwa (1772). These periods expired, and permission was granted again as in the past for twenty years beginning with the next year of the rat (1852), as ordered in the tenth month, fourth year of Kaei (1851).

23. As the late Hyōuemon and the late Yahei of the fishing village in Fukuyama district were particularly commendable for providing relief rice and other goods when Sakurajima erupted, their successive heirs shall be permitted the use of surnames, and they shall be of the same status as Kagoshima townsmen, as ordered in the first month, sixth year of Temmei (1786).

24. As the late Suda Gihei of the fishing village of Uchinoura provided emergency rice and other goods throughout the village, by special consideration of the daimyo his successive heirs shall be granted the use of the surname.

25. Because there were few people in the fishing village of Ōka-wa in Konejime district, upon their request, marriage reciprocity with peasants within their district was granted from time to time for twenty-year periods beginning with the second year of Temmei (1782). However, the periods expired, and upon further petition, permission was granted as in the past for a period of thirty years beginning with the fourteenth year of Tempō (1843).

26. Because the fishing village of Shirahama in Tōgō district was in a situation similar to the above, upon their petition, mar-riage reciprocity with rural townsmen and peasants residing within the same district was granted to them for fifteen years, beginning with the eighth month, seventh year of Temmei (1787). However, in the seventh month, second year of Kyōwa (1802) the period expired, and upon further petition, permission was granted again for twenty years beginning with the sixth year of Bunsei (1823). This period expired in the thirteenth year of Tempō (1842).

27. The town of Komenotsu in Izumi district gradually became poorer and its population diminished. Therefore, upon petition, the residents were granted a twenty-year period of marriage rec-iprocity with peasants and rural townspeople within their district, beginning with the third month, twelfth year of Kansei (1800). However, the period expired in the second year of Bunsei (1819). Upon further petition, permission was granted again for twenty years as in the past beginning with the sixth year of Bunsei (1823). This period expired in the thirteenth year of Tempō (1842).

28. The late Hamazaki Taheiji of the fishing village of Mina-toura in Ibusuki district and Yoshizaki Yauemon of the fishing village of Surinohama in the same district have been particularly meritorious in their conduct. In addition, they performed well a variety of services on each occasion of the daimyo's visit to Ibu-suki. Thus, by the daimyo's special consideration, they were permitted to have surnames on a hereditary basis in the second month, sixth year of Kansei (1794). In the fourth month, twelfth year of the same year period, it was announced that members of their families down to the youngest son shall record their sur-names.

29. Because the fishing village of Machihama in Konejime dis-trict became impoverished, upon petition, the residents were twice

granted permission to bring in by marriage peasants from within their own district, permission being for twenty years each time, beginning with the twelfth year of Kansei (1800). When the periods expired, upon further petition, permission was granted again as in the past for twenty years beginning with the eleventh year of Tempō (1840).

30. Nayamachi in Chōsa district is a semi-fishing village [*han ura*]. Because the residents were poor and few in number they had difficulty arranging marriages appropriate to their station, and the population gradually decreased. They thus petitioned for marriage reciprocity not only with the rural townsmen of Nayamachi in Chōsa district but also with the people of the semi-fishing village of Tōkamachi, and of the fishing village of Matsubara and of the farm village of Shioya, all in Chōsa district. Permission was granted as petitioned twice since the twelfth year of Bunka (1815) for specified periods. These periods expired, and upon further petition, permission was granted again as in the past for ten years beginning with the second year of Kōka (1845).

31. As for the townsmen in Shibushi district, only those who hold residential land and who are heads of households may call themselves *myōzu* and use surnames as in the past. Those who have residential land, but who do not have surnames for the time being, shall use surnames as stated above. Town officials shall be permitted to use surnames for the period of their service only. Others who have been using the *myōzu* title or using surnames without knowing how they acquired them shall not use surnames hereafter, as ordered in the second month, twelfth year of Bunka (1815).

32. Though half of the rural town of Tōkamachi in Chōsa district had been permitted to become a semi-fishing village, now upon further petition, the whole community shall be permitted to become a semi-fishing village and the people shall be allowed to marry residents of other fishing villages, as ordered in the third month, twelfth year of Bunka (1815).

33. Because the fishing village of Hishida in Ōsaki district was poor, upon their request, marriage reciprocity with rural townsmen and with peasants residing within the district was granted to the residents for a ten-year period beginning with the twelfth year of Bunka (1815). The period expired, and in the eighth year of

Bunsei (1825) for ten years thereafter permission was granted to bring in by marriage rural townsmen and peasants within the district. However, the period expired, and an extension was granted as in the past for ten years beginning with the eighth year of Tempō (1837). This period expired in the third year of Kōka (1846).

34. Because the fishing villagers in Yoshitoshi district were unable to arrange marriages appropriate to their station, they were granted marriage reciprocity with peasants residing in their own district for twenty years, as ordered in the fifth month, twelfth year of Kansei (1800). The period expired in the second year of Bunsei (1819).

35. The late Koreeda Sukeemon and Koreeda Sukejūrō of the town of Matsuzaki in Taniyama district, being apprised of the difficult times for the daimyo, donated a sum of money. By special consideration of the daimyo they were granted permission to use surnames for one generation, whereupon this time they presented the daimyo with money as an expression of gratitude. For their second praiseworthy thoughtfulness they were granted the use of a surname on a hereditary basis, as ordered in the first month, fifteenth year of Bunka (1818).

36. Residents of the fishing villages of Takame and Sezaki in Imaizumi district, upon their petition, were granted permission to bring in rural townspeople by marriage. When the period expired, and upon further petition, as of the ninth year of Bunsei (1826), they were repeatedly granted marriage reciprocity for specified periods with peasants and rural townspeople within their own district. These periods having expired, and upon further petitions, they were granted from the fourth year of Kōka (1847) a ten-year period of marriage reciprocity with peasants and rural townspeople residing not only within their own district but also in the districts of Taniyama, Kiire, Ibusuki, Yamagawa, Ei, Chiran, and Kago.

37. Since Eguchihama, Akazakiura, and Kannokawaura in Ichiki district were generally poor fishing villages their residents had difficulty arranging marriages appropriate to their station. Upon their petition, therefore, from the second year of Kōka (1845) for a period of ten years they were granted marriage reciprocity with peasants residing in their own district.

38. Because the several fishing villages in Ei district were poor, upon petition, for a period of ten years beginning with the eighth year of Bunsei (1825), the villagers were granted marriage reciprocity with peasants and rural townspeople residing in their own district as well as in the neighboring districts of Chiran, Kago, Kawanabe, Yamada in Kawanabe county, Kiire, Ibusuki, Yamagawa, and Imaizumi. When the period expired, permission was extended as in the past for twenty years beginning with the eighth year of Tempō (1837).

39. Because the fishing villages of Kadonoura, Matsugaura, Nishishioyaura and Higashishioyaura in Chiran district were especially impoverished, their residents were unable to arrange marriage reciprocity within these communities. Upon petition, since the first year of Bunsei (1818), periods of ten years each were granted twice for marriage reciprocity with peasants residing not only within their own district but also in the neighboring districts of Ei, Kawanabe, Yamada in Kawanabe county, and Kago. These periods expired, and upon further petition, in the first year of Kaei (1848) a ten-year period was granted for marriage reciprocity with peasants residing not only within their own district but also in the neighboring districts of Ei, Kawanabe, Yamada in Kawanabe county, Kago, and Kaseda.

40. In the case of the town of Hamanoichi in Kokubu district, by special consideration of the daimyo for its distinguished history, the use of surnames was granted to the *toshigyōji* when they retired after a completely satisfactory period of service and to the heads of *myōzu* households. Moreover, even though the title of *myōzu* has been used in the past by second and third sons of *myōzu* who establish branch families and render services for the *han,* and by individuals who once held residential land but who do not now hold such land, the term *myōzu* shall be restricted to those who presently hold residential land, even though it be a parcel of such land. In order to avoid confusion in the future this regulation was promulgated in the ninth month, first year of Kyōwa (1801).

41. Residents of the fishing village of Hami in Kōyama district, though few in number, have been rendering the same services to the *han* as other fishing villages. However, because they were very poor, arranging marriages with other fishing villages was difficult.

Upon their petition, marriage reciprocity with rural townsmen and peasants within their own district and in neighboring districts was granted in the thirteenth year of Bunsei (1830) for a period of ten years thereafter. This period expired, and again in the second year of Kōka (1845) permission was extended as in the past for ten years thereafter.

42. Because the residents of the fishing village of Kashiwabaru in Kushira district were poor, they were unable to arrange marriages appropriate to their station. Upon their request, for a period of ten years, beginning with the next year of the dog (1838), permission was granted to bring in by marriage rural townspeople and peasants residing in their own district and in the districts of Kōyama and Ōsaki, as ordered on the thirteenth day, eighth month, eighth year of Tempō (1837).

43. In the case of the fishing village of Hamamura in Kokubu district, by special consideration of the daimyo for its old distinguished history, the use of surnames is granted to *benzashi* when they retire after a fully satisfactory period of service and to heads of *ura myōzu* households, as ordered in the second month, fourth year of Tempō (1833).

44. The fishing village of Kannokawa in Ijūin district being extremely poor and especially small in population, its residents have been unable to arrange marriages appropriate to their station. Upon their petition, for a period of ten years, beginning with the second year of Kōka (1845) they were granted marriage reciprocity with peasants residing within their own district and in the districts of Hioki and Ichiki.

45. Because Ōsaki in Kaseda district was a poor fishing village, its residents were unable to arrange marriages appropriate to their station. Upon their petition, they were granted marriage reciprocity with peasants residing within their own district and in the districts of Mizuhiki and Taniyama for a period of three years, beginning with the third year of Kōka (1846). This period expired in the first year of Kaei (1848).

XVII. Regulations on the inspection of tags of persons registered in other people's households, relatives of violators of the *han* laws, and runaways

1. As to castle-town samurai, *gōshi,* and others who are permitted by status to use surnames, when there is a petition by relatives for admission into their households for whatever reason, an investigation shall be made each time, and those of good lineage shall be admitted into the households. They shall record their surnames both on their tags and in the register. Those whose household tags are not of good lineage to begin with, shall be issued tags without surnames as heretofore. Those who do not know about their past status shall be recorded as attached to the relative's household, and they shall all be without surnames.

Proviso: A person without a surname shall be permitted to leave for fixed periods of employment with various categories of commoners. Because of the possible confusion that [such a person] was adopted by a person whose status permits him the use of a surname, a side notation shall be entered on the tag and in the register that originally he was of the household of so-and-so. The marriage of a daughter [of a person] in the above category shall conform to the marriage [regulation] for daughters of servants of the various categories of commoners and they shall not be allowed to marry others [except as provided by the above provision].

2. Castle-town samurai and *gōshi,* who have violated the *han* law, and runaways shall be stripped of their samurai status. Members of their households shall be removed from the [samurai] unit

register and from the register of land stipends. Those who are placed in the household of relatives, shall not be allowed to be adopted as heirs, to establish branch households, or to be assigned to official service. If the status of the above people is not clear, those who have been using surnames may continue to do so if they wish, but they must record their ages and enter a side notation on their tags and in the register, "former relative of so-and-so."

Proviso: Anyone shall be permitted to employ these people as male or female servants by obtaining a verifying statement from their former household. It is strictly forbidden to revise their tags on a permanent basis. Moreover, their status in the employer's household shall be determined at the discretion of the employer. Daughters [of persons] in the above category shall not be permitted to marry castle-town samurai or *gōshi*.

3. When those of *yoriki* rank and below, who have recorded their surnames, violate the *han* laws as stated above, the members of their household, being their relatives, shall each be deprived of their status and shall be issued tags including them in the household of relatives. They shall not have surnames, and on their tags and in the register they shall enter a side notation, "formerly relative of so-and-so."

Proviso: The above people shall be in the same category as servants of various categories of commoners, and without exception, they are prohibited from being adopted or married by one who is permitted to record his surname.

4. Household members of a person charged with violation of *han* laws who are assigned to be wards of a relative, shall not be transferred to some other household.

Proviso: If there is an imperative reason, upon their petition, [these wards] shall be allowed to be transferred.

5. Castle-town samurai and *gōshi* who ran away and returned shall be reported. Unless there are special circumstances, they shall lose their surnames and be placed in the household of a relative.

6. When a person who ran away and returned requests a tag, a petition shall be submitted to the office of the magistrate for tag inspection with a statement in legal form including when and by whom his return was reported.

Proviso: A runaway who has returned shall record on his tag and in the register, "returned runaway; forbidden to depart for other domains."

7. As for runaways, a record shall be entered into the register of household inspection as to when and by whom the disappearance was reported. The tags [of the runaway] shall be confiscated.

8. During the period that a samurai, who has been stripped of his status, is in exile on a distant island without pardon, his wife, children, and [other] household members shall receive tags as members of a relative's household, even though they may not be required to be in the relative's custody.

Proviso: After the wife and children of the person exiled to an island have been excused from the custody of relatives, the children shall be issued tags with their status being determined by the given situation.

XVIII. Regulations on the inspection of tags of employees from the Kyoto-Osaka area and of residents from other domains

1. Those who are from the Kyoto-Osaka area for term employment, those temporarily residing [for employment] in the *han,* those residing permanently, and other men and women from other domains who reside within our *han,* shall obtain their first tags with verifying statements from the office of term employment.

Proviso: They shall enter side notations on their tags stating whether they are here for term employment, temporary residence, or permanent settlement, and from which domain they came, and by whom they are employed.

2. The above-mentioned people and those who have been in permanent residence for a long while and who have been issued tags in the past, shall be issued tags similar to their old ones.

3. It was the law of the domain that those who came from the Kyoto-Osaka area for permanent employment should not change their household of tag registration to any other except that of the employer's parents, children, or brothers. However, since the temporary residents may change their employer at their discretion, permanent employees from the Kyoto-Osaka area, by mutual agreement, may also change their employers in the same way as temporary residents, as ordered in the tenth month, fourth year of An'ei (1775).

4. When a person, whose term of employment is completed, and who has no one in the Kyoto-Osaka area responsible for him, peti-

tions for temporary residence in the *han*, his employer shall make the request to the office for term employment. Pending the decision he shall request a tag with a supporting statement from the office for term employment.

Proviso: Later, when the matter is settled, and he is issued a tag, a written statement from the office for term employment shall be required.

5. When employees from the Kyoto-Osaka area die, or when they return home after completion of their term of employment, all such cases shall be recorded in the register of household inspection, and their tags shall be retrieved.

6. A permanent employee from the Kyoto-Osaka area who, because of a crime, is assigned to be the servant of a peasant in any of the districts, shall record the name of his former employer permanently both on his tag and in the register. Of course, he shall also record the name of his present employer both on his tag and in the register.

7. If a child is born to a traveler bearing documents of an agent of a commission firm, the traveler shall report the circumstances in legal form to the office of the magistrate for tag inspection, and the case shall be investigated.

8. Daughters of temporary residents [for employment] in our domain shall be permitted entry or departure for marriage in the same way as for daughters of our townsmen. However, when they revise their tags they shall submit documents written by the town magistrate, by the maritime magistrate, and by their employers.

9. When those who are recorded in the master register of gold mines are to be permanently employed by castle-town samurai or by subretainers, the magistrate of gold mines shall report to the department of economy, and after receipt of official permission, employment shall begin. Therefore, hereafter the statement of the office of the magistrate of tag inspection shall not be required, but their tags shall be revised on the basis of the verifying statement written by the magistrate of gold mines.

Proviso: When they are permanently employed by samurai, they and their descendants shall write a side notation stating their home domain and the fact that they are recorded in the master register of gold mines.

10. Miners residing at the two gold mines located in the districts of Yamagano and Kago are not so recorded in the master register at this time, but they are only listed as *hitokerai*. Since this procedure is inconvenient for the mining operation, all those who heretofore were of the status of *hitokerai* shall change their status at this time, and shall be listed as "gold miners" assigned to the office of the magistrate of gold mines. Their social status shall be the same as that of people assigned to the magistrate of finance. Both on their tags and in the register they shall record their surnames and their ages, and in side notations they shall state their domain of origin and the fact that they are recorded in the master register of gold mines. They shall be permitted to marry people of *ashigaru* or lower status. *Gōshi* of the various districts, while residing away from home for purposes of employment in the gold mines, also shall be under the supervision of the magistrate of gold mines during their period of work, and they shall be excused from their various service obligations and monetary contributions in their respective districts. It is ordered that in all matters they are responsible to the magistrate of gold mines. Henceforth people who enter from other domains as [gold mine] workers shall be recorded in the master register [of gold mines]. Moreover, the same procedure as for the gold mines shall apply in all matters relating to the tin mine in Taniyama district. The above regulations were ordered in the third month, third year of Bunsei (1820).

11. Because of their small number, residents at the Yamagano gold mine area, who are under the jurisdiction of the office of the magistrate of gold mines, had difficulty arranging marriages appropriate to their station. Upon their petition, therefore, for a period of twenty years beginning with the twelfth year of Tempō (1841) they were permitted marriage reciprocity with *gōshi* and others of lower status residing in the districts of Yokogawa, Honjō, Yunoo, Magoshi, Soki, Mizobe, Kurino, and Odori, as ordered in the first month, twelfth year of Tempō (1841).

12. Because of their small number, residents at the Kago gold mine, who are in the same category as above, had difficulty arranging marriages appropriate to their station. Upon their request, therefore, for a period of twenty years beginning with the twelfth year of Tempō (1841), they were permitted marriage re-

ciprocity with people of *gōshi* and lower status residing in the districts of Kaseda, Bōdomari, Yamada in Kawanabe county, Kawanabe, Kushiakime, and Ata, as ordered in the first month, twelfth year of Tempō (1841).

13. Because of their small number, residents at the Taniyama tin mine, who are in the same category as above, had difficulty arranging marriages appropriate to their station. Upon their request, therefore, for a period of twenty years beginning with the twelfth year of Tempō (1841) they were permitted marriage reciprocity with people of *gōshi* and lower status residing in the districts of Taniyama, Izaku, Tabuse, Ata, and Kawanabe, as ordered in the first month, twelfth year of Tempō (1841).

XIX. Regulations on the inspection of tags of those exiled by the Bakufu and of people from other domains

1. Those exiled by the Bakufu who are obtaining their tags for the first time shall have their custodian act in their behalf, and the tag shall be issued on the basis of a written statement of verification by the *han* steward.

Proviso: A side notation shall be entered on the tag indicating [the exile's] domain of origin and the name of his custodian. Also when the custodian is changed, a written statement of verification by the *han* steward shall be required for the revision of the exile's tag.

2. When an exile is pardoned, dies, or escapes, the retrieval of the tag shall also be on the basis of a verifying statement by the *han* steward.

3. If a person of another domain has lived for several years in our domain and has wandered about through several districts without having received a tag, upon cross-examination, he shall divulge fully to the local *gōshi* elder or *yakunin* the domain from whence he came and the year of his arrival in the *han*. This shall be reported to the office of the magistrate for tag inspection.

XX. Regulations on the inspection of tags of persons who have incurred the daimyo's displeasure or who have been imprisoned or exiled to distant islands

1. Castle-town samurai, *gōshi, ashigaru,* the lord's errand runners, the lord's grooms, and the lord's teahouse attendants, who are deprived of their respective statuses due to the displeasure of the daimyo, shall obtain tags of the household of a relative or of any other person they wish. They shall omit their surnames from their tags and from the register, but they shall record their ages. Of course, the same provisions shall apply to their wives and children and to members of their households.

Proviso: Persons in the above situation shall apply at the office of the magistrate for tag inspection bringing statements on legal forms written by the people who are taking them into their households.

2. The remaining members of the household of a castle-town samurai or *gōshi* who has been exiled to an island need not be assigned to the household of a relative, but they shall receive their tags as they have in the past.

Proviso: When persons attached to offices, *hitokerai,* shrine personnel, temple-gate personnel, peasants, fishermen, and townsmen, are exiled to distant islands, those among their relatives who are informed that they are not included [in the punishment] shall fill in the register and request tags as above.

3. An island exile, or a person residing on an island by petition [of others], shall have recorded in his household register the month

and year and by whom he was ordered banished, and his tag shall be taken from him.

4. Persons exiled to distant islands shall apply for tags at the island of exile, and their old tags shall be taken from them.

Proviso: A samurai who has been deprived of his status and exiled to a distant island shall omit his surname from his tag, but he shall record his age. A samurai who has not been deprived of his status shall record his surname as in the past.

5. An island exile, or a person residing on an island by petition [of others], upon being pardoned, shall request a tag by reporting to the office of the magistrate for tag inspection with a statement on legal form setting forth the month and year and by whom he is ordered to be pardoned.

Proviso: The old tag issued at the island of exile shall be brought forth.

6. An island exile, or a person residing on an island by petition [of others], who requests a tag, and upon being pardoned, unwittingly returns home without the above tag and does not produce it within a five-year period, shall be fined three hundred *mon* for his absent-minded withholding of tag. The new tag shall be retained at the office of the magistrate for tag inspection, or sometimes at the office of accounting. When the island tag is turned in, it shall be exchanged for the new one, as ordered in the fourth month, twelfth year of Kansei (1800).

7. When an island exile is pardoned, or when a person is ordered to be released from prison, the status which is to be recorded on his tag will depend on the circumstances of each case.

8. A person in prison who has been given no information concerning the disposition of his case shall have a relative pick up his tag. Moreover, the above person's wife and children and members of his household also shall obtain their tags through a relative.

Proviso: If he does not have relatives, the person having jurisdiction over him shall obtain the tags.

9. When a castle-town samurai or *gōshi* is imprisoned for an offense, and his daughter has married into another household, if she is requesting a revision of her tag for the first time, she must obtain instructions on the procedure for receiving the tag pending disposition of her father's case.

10. When a person is banished to a distant island for some offense, his tag and those of his household members shall be sealed by the police inspector and placed in charge of a relative. The tags shall be kept under seal and presented to the authorities, who shall examine them in the usual manner. Moreover, if a person is in the custody of a relative for a crime which does not call for deprivation of status, he shall not be required to become a member of the relative's household, and he shall be issued a tag as in the past. Of course, when a person is deprived of his status and placed in the custody of a relative, as in the past he shall take the various steps necessary to petition the officials for inclusion into the relative's household. These regulations were promulgated in the eighth month, ninth year of Tempō (1838).

XXI. Regulations for checking all types of tags

1. Careful attention shall be given during inspection to such matters as lost tags, burned tags, stolen tags, and tags with wrong sex designation. If there are no irregularities, documents to that effect shall be verified, and a new tag shall be issued. Since lost tags and tags with the wrong sex designation are the result of carelessness, a fine shall be levied in accordance with previous regulations. In addition, tags shall be examined minutely for such things as scraping the face of the tag, rewriting the characters, forging tags, or substituting tags. When there are any cases of carelessness with tags, the details shall be reported and exposed.

2. If a tag is placed in pawn and this becomes an obstacle to marriage reciprocity the tag must be returned to the original owner regardless of secret understandings to the contrary. Because [the original owner] must obtain a new tag, his [old] tag shall be returned to him. If after obtaining his new tag, the person does not return it to the person who has custody, the latter shall report this fact to the office of the magistrate for tag inspection.

3. Hereafter it shall be forbidden to scrape a little to rewrite words which are erroneously written at the time the tag is being prepared because such a practice may cause future difficulties. In the above situation the entire surface of the tag shall be [scraped and] rewritten.

4. After comparing the old tags with the old register the old

tags shall be obliterated and the inspecting official shall hand them back to each of the individuals. Each person shall plane his own tag and return it. If the tag becomes too thin, he shall be instructed to prepare a new one.

Proviso: When people die they shall be listed on a separate sheet of paper which shall be submitted [to the authorities].

5. As in previous tag inspections, the purpose of the inspection of religious sects shall be written into the foreword of the register for the five-man associations, the seal impression of each person shall be obtained, and a separate copy shall be made and submitted to the authorities.

6. It was ordered recently that the records of persons departing or entering [the district] should be mutually exchanged [between districts] and corrected. Upon their submission, the records shall be compared with the register. If there are no discrepancies, fair copies shall be made in the register immediately. Since it would take extra days to perfect registers care should be taken not to waste time on unnecessary details. Moreover, as many districts must be inspected by a single team, the number of days which were required to complete one district shall be submitted to the office of the magistrate for tag inspection. If an excessive number of days is taken there shall surely be a reprimand.

Proviso: A written report shall be submitted for the number of days taken for the locally conducted inspection.

7. Although an order was issued recently to complete tag inspections without delay, if the delay is caused by [the tardy exchange of] the record of departures and entries of people, the inspection officials shall obtain instructions from the magistrate of tag inspection.

8. The following information shall be accurately recorded on the tag: day, month, and year [of inspection], the person's name and age, and the name of his master if he has one; in addition, townspeople and peasants shall indicate that they are so-and-so from such-and-such town or village.

9. Above one's name on the tag and in the register the person's religious sect shall be recorded accurately. When a child is born the religious sect of the parents shall be recorded for the child in the same manner as above.

10. Persons who were left out of the last inspection and did not receive tags should become aware of this omission after the inspection, so they shall report the fact immediately. If they conceal the fact and are exposed by others, then their master or supervisory head, or the *gōshi* elders in the case of the district, or the *yakunin* [of the private domain], shall be responsible for the oversight.

11. Since it is likely that there will be an official inquiry about a person's movements from his place of registration and his later destination, care must be taken in the inspection not to overlook any tags. Particularly persons who, when requesting tags, produce documents pasted together consecutively, and persons who are divested of tags, shall record in the [household] register of their present master that in the year of the serpent (1845), they were registered in the household of so-and-so. The departures and entries of the above types of people shall be investigated with care.

XXII. Regulations and legal procedures for meting out fines

1. If a person scrapes off the side notation, "formerly Ikkō sect," from the face of his tag, he shall be fined one piece of silver [*ichi mai*]. Moreover, if the tag has an Ikkō sect side notation, the district inspector shall impress his seal upon it and instruct the bearer to be careful that the characters do not fade away.

2. Persons who fail to obtain their tags in time shall be fined after the inspection one *kammon* per inspection.

3. A person who loses his tag in a shipwreck en route to the Ryukyus or other islands shall not be fined if there are no discrepancies [in his report] at the time of his return to Satsuma. However, if the person fails to report [his loss] at the time of his return, and he submits his report after thirty-six months have elapsed, he shall be fined five hundred *mon* copper, as ordered in the ninth month, seventh year of Bunsei (1824).

4. A person who has lost his tag, but who has proof of his loss, shall be fined two hundred *mon* copper. If he does not have such proof, he shall be fined five hundred *mon* copper.

Proviso: A person whose tag has been stolen, or who takes a tag with the sex erroneously recorded, shall be fined five hundred *mon* copper.

5. When the characters are illegible because the face of the tag is worm-eaten, or because it is smeared, the fine shall be three hundred *mon* copper. The tag shall be confiscated, and a special

report shall be submitted, as ordered in the fourth month, twelfth year of Bunka (1815).

6. A person who has lost his tag in a fire, or by some other unforeseen misfortune, shall be fined five hundred *mon* copper.

Proviso: No fine shall be levied against a person who has proof of such loss, but if he does not report [immediately] after the incident, but he does so after twelve months have elapsed, he shall be fined five hundred *mon* copper, as ordered in the ninth month, seventh year of Bunsei (1824).

7. A person who has requested a "true child" tag for a foster child shall be fined two *kammon* copper.

Proviso: The true father of the above child shall be fined five hundred *mon* copper.

8. A fine of two hundred fifty *mon* copper each: When the above infraction is by *gōshi* or subretainers in private domains, the fine shall be levied as above against the individual's [samurai] unit and unit chief if the unit is guilty of carelessness; against the *toshiyori,* *toshigyōji,* and *myōzu* if the offending person is a townsman; against the *shōya, nanushi,* and [five-man] association if the offending person is a peasant; and additionally [against local responsible officials when] temple-gate personnel and fishing villagers are involved.

Proviso: It was announced in the third month, year of the dog [1790, 1802, 1814?] that, in cases involving domiciliary confinement or restriction of movement, the fine shall be paid in silver by the *gōshi* elder, the unit chief, and the [offending] *gōshi* when the jurisdictional unit is the district, and by the *yakunin* when the jurisdictional unit is the private domain. However, when the case involves a tag inspection official, the fine shall be paid in copper.

9. The secret employment of daughters of peasants, townsmen, fishermen, and temple-gate personnel as a way of paying off the interest on a debt shall be forbidden. If a woman is employed as a day laborer and as a way of paying interest on a debt, and, in the course of events, she gives birth to a child, the child shall be assigned to the mother. Since the above situation is in violation of the *han* law, both parents shall be fined one *kammon* copper each.

Proviso: If a peasant, townsman, fisherman, or a temple-gate personnel member, while secretly employed as a day laborer, has relations with a maid servant of a castle-town samurai and begets a child, the child shall be assigned to its father. Since such an affair is in violation of the *han* law, both parents shall be fined as above.

10. If a daughter of a peasant, rural townsman, fisherman, or temple-gate personnel is employed without a written permit, and she gives birth to a child, both parents shall be fined one *kammon* copper each.

11. If a child of a peasant is secretly adopted by someone in violation of the *han* law, both parents shall be fined two *kammon* copper each.

Proviso: The above child shall be returned to the peasant.

12. A peasant or rural townsman who pawns his tag shall be fined seventy stakes.

13. A fine of fifty wooden stakes each: In the above case, those who stand surety and members of the five-man association shall be fined in kind as stipulated above.

14. A fine of seventy wooden stakes: In the above case, if the *toshigyōji* or *bettō* in the rural town had knowledge of the affair, they shall be fined in kind as stipulated above, the same as the offending person.

15. A fine of three hundred *mon* copper: In the above case, if the person standing surety is someone other than a peasant, the above people shall pay the fine in copper.

Proviso: A *gōshi* serving as *shōya* or *bettō,* who had knowledge that the tag was placed in pawn, should be fined in copper, and he should seek further instructions. The fine shall not apply to *shōya, toshigyōji,* and *bettō* who had no knowledge of the above situation.

16. A fine of one hundred fifty wooden stakes: When a person secretly retains a woman from a peasant village or rural town instead of returning her to her original *kado* after her term of employment had expired, and he begets a child by her, he shall be fined in kind as stipulated above. Of course, if the *shōya* or *bettō* is culpable the same penalty shall apply.

17. A fine of one hundred stakes each: For the above offense, members of the offender's [five-man] association shall be fined in kind.

18. If a peasant goes to a *kengo* or *eta* village for marriage or adoption, both parties shall be fined one piece of silver.

19. If in the inspection of the tags there is a blunder in whatever manner, an appropriate fine shall be assessed even though the person guilty be a castle-town samurai, *gōshi*, or a priest in charge of a temple.

20. Anyone who scrapes away or rewrites the characters on the tag, even if done in ignorance or by a child, shall be fined one piece of silver. If the above abuse was due to the innocent act of a child, his parent, brother, or other relative who is responsible for him, shall pay the fine.

21. Trifling mistakes in writing unimportant characters on the tag shall not be cause for censure. However, if the mistakes be repeated with many people, or if they involve such matters as the recording of ages or the writing of side notations, not only the clerk but also the inspecting officials shall be charged with an offense.

XXIII. Miscellaneous

1. When it is reported that the old tag is unavailable because the person carried it with him overseas to Ryukyu or to other islands, the matter shall be carefully investigated, and if there are no irregularities a new tag shall be kept for him at the inspection office. When the person returns, the old tag shall be taken away and the new tag shall be issued to him. If the office of the magistrate for tag inspection has already concluded its work, the old tag shall be turned in to the office of *han* accounting; a new tag shall be issued to him, and this fact shall be reported.

Proviso: An abstract shall be entered in a separate book listing such persons, and it shall be submitted to the office of the magistrate for tag inspection.

2. If there is any suspicion about the manner in which tags for foster children of the various categories of commoners were obtained, a careful investigation shall be made, and if there is no basis for doubt, the tags shall be issued as in the past.

3. Since the characters for *yashinaigo* ("foster child") can be confused with those for *yōshi* ("adopted child"), the phonetic symbol, *hi*, shall be inserted between the two characters for *yashinaigo*, as ordered in the fifth month, fourth year of Bunsei (1821).

4. Among *ashigaru,* the lord's grooms, the lord's errand runners, the lord's teahouse attendants, peasants, rural townsmen, fishermen, shrine personnel, temple-gate personnel, and attendants and

servants of samurai, there are those who are ambiguous about the birth of children. In such cases, the parents shall be questioned whether the child is indeed their true child. All children born after the previous inspection shall be carefully examined so that there are no omissions, and new tags shall be issued to them. A tag shall be issued even for those who are away [from Satsuma].

Proviso: If the parents are under different jurisdiction or serve different masters, each shall provide the facts in written reports.

5. Obtaining household tags for people who are not one's hereditary attendants or servants in disregard of one's social status, and placing a large number of these people in various localities, cause difficulties for rural towns and agricultural villages. Such actions have been long forbidden. If there are people who request an inappropriate number of tags, special instructions shall be obtained from the office of the magistrate for tag inspection.

6. When the tag inspection has been completed and the new tags are being issued, all males among the various categories of commoners shall personally come forth to receive their tags. Especially the males among peasants, townspeople, and fishing villagers shall all be summoned, and as in the past they shall be issued tags as each person is verified.

7. When there are people who have not been assigned to any jurisdiction, the law provides that they shall become peasants. When there are such people a report shall be made to the authorities.

Proviso: In the past, people in the above category were called "floating people." They shall be examined with care.

8. If a person has been forced to leave his village because of an offense, his daughter shall not be permitted to marry anyone in her father's original village.

9. It has long been forbidden for anyone to secretly employ runaways or people from other domains. Because there may be such people being secretly harbored, care shall be exercised in the investigation. Of course, depending upon the circumstances, they shall be arrested, and a report shall be made to the authorities.

10. People who are permanently stationed in Edo, or who reside in Kyoto or Osaka, shall not be required to carry tags. They shall be listed in the register for religious census, which shall be

submitted to and kept in the tag inspection office. At the time of the next inspection, a check shall be made with the information in the register.

11. At the next tag inspection, upon due investigation, tags shall be seized belonging to any castle-town samurai and *gōshi*, and including the lowest member of society, male and female, whose whereabouts are unaccountably unknown, or who were on board a ship which has not been sighted, and about which there has been no information for many years. If by some chance, they should return in some later year, they shall be issued new tags.

12. People residing in Nagasaki, as in the case of those residing in Kyoto and Osaka, shall not be required to carry tags. They shall be listed in the register for religious census which shall be submitted to the authorities, as ordered in the ninth month, third year of Kōka (1846).

13. According to law, when, for some offense committed by castle-town samurai, their attendants or servants are placed in custody as *agarimono,* those of *yoriai* rank or higher who request their custody shall be denied. Moreover, after a person has won custody of the above *agarimono* by lot, the latter may not later be transferred permanently to some other household. However, when the custodian dies and his wards have no master, upon petition, custody may be shifted to some other party.

14. Keepers of falcons have been assigned to various areas and allowed to establish households. But since it was difficult to arrange marriages limited to their category, the warden of falcons petitioned for marriage reciprocity with peasants and townsmen. Consequently permission for marriage reciprocity with peasants and townsmen is granted together with permission for reciprocity in adoptions. Moreover, falcon keepers are peasants, and in these families the duty of falcon keeper is assigned from heir to heir. In these families, if a person, though he be the youngest son, is outstanding as falcon keeper and thus useful to the lord, he shall be appointed as falcon keeper. However, as a general rule, second and younger sons shall be made peasants. The district officials shall exercise judgment in assigning them suitable, vacant rice fields so that they can devote themselves to agriculture. Younger sons who remain in the household of the falcon keeper shall obtain

permission from the warden of falcons when they depart for such reasons as term employment. After they become peasants, they shall be treated like other peasants, the above being ordered in the fourth month, seventh year of Kansei (1795).

15. Those who are ordered to reside in Yakushima and Tanega-shima, or who have been sent to Yakushima as punishment, shall request their new tags at their place of domicile, as ordered in the sixth month, twelfth year of Bunka (1815).

XXIV. Regulations on the inspection of tags of *kengo*, *eta*, and *angya*

1. The tags of *kengo, eta,* and *angya* shall have the seal impressed sideways.

Proviso: *Kengo* and *eta* who have had seals impressed upright in the past shall follow the same procedure as in the past, but the servants of *kengo* and *eta* shall have the seal impressed sideways.

2. Men or women who become *angya* and withdraw from their households shall submit supporting statements written by their neighbors or by their supervisor, if they have one, and shall have their names removed from the register.

3. Among *hinin* who travel about to various places, there are confusing cases of persons whose family background is unknown, who subsist by begging, and who do not carry tags. Although according to law those who are not under any specific jurisdiction shall be assigned to become peasants, if it is determined upon investigation that a beggar, who was ordered to become a peasant, has been useless, he shall receive his tag from the *eta* community of his district, as ordered in the tenth month of the third year of Bunsei (1820).

4. As to Fujimoto Hikoroku, the *myōzu* of the *eta* community of Kamiemura in Iino district, his ancestors were granted the surname of Fujimoto because they rendered specially meritorious service to the daimyo. However, the use of the surname was discontinued. Now, upon petition and by special consideration of the

daimyo, he and his heirs for two generations shall be granted the use of the surname and the privilege of stamping the seal upright on their tags, as ordered in the twelfth month, eleventh year of Tempō (1840).

The aforementioned articles shall be strictly upheld and the tag inspection shall be carried out with care. In addition to the above, if there is any matter which is not understood, one should obtain instructions from the office of magistrate for tag inspection as often as needed. For matters concerning the district and private domain, the *gōshi* elders and *yakunin* respectively shall be consulted for the inspection. If there is any carelessness, it shall be punished with certainty, so there shall be no laxness.

Magistrates for Tag Inspection
Niiro Kura
Hongō Danri
First month, fifth year of Kaei (1852)
Honda Rokuzaemon
Ei Oribe

Part 3
GLOSSARY

GLOSSARY

agarimono   An attendant of a samurai criminal who was seized and reduced to slave status by the authorities.

angya   A wandering mendicant who was of quasi-outcaste status.

ashigaru   A footman or foot-soldier whose status was below that of quasi-samurai.

benzashi   A fishing village assistant head, who was elected from among the *ura-myōzu*. Equivalent to *nanushi* in agricultural village.

bettō   The head of a rural town, appointed in principle from among *gōshi*.

buichiyama   A mountain or waste field area afforested with or without the *han* government permission. If permission was acquired, the timber harvest was shared equally between the government and the forester. If prior permission was not obtained, the forester retained one-third of the timber crop.

chakuza   The privilege of having an assigned seat at the audience given by the daimyo.

eta   See *hinin*.

gejo   A woman servant.

genin   A servant (usually refers to a male). The *Jōmoku* refers to *genin* with *genin* tag. There were, however, other *genin* who were without such tag and were not reported as *genin*.

go-ichimon   A rank bestowed upon the four member houses of the Satsuma daimyo who were legally and socially treated as the relatives of the Satsuma daimyo.

gosanke   Three junior houses of the Tokugawa family, Owari, Kii, and Mito, each descended from sons of the founding shogun, Tokugawa Ieyasu. Their principal duties were to assist the main Tokugawa House and to supply an heir in case the main line failed to produce an heir.

gōshi   From the late eighteenth century (*ca.* 1780–83) samurai residents in rural areas were called *gōshi* (rural samurai). Some

149

of them had stipends but many received very little and had to support themselves by agriculture.

gōshi meshitsukai   A servant employed by *gōshi*.

go-yōnin or *yōnin*   A liaison official between the councilor and lesser officials. Until about 1673–80 he was variously called *mōshi-guchiyaku, mōshitsugiyaku*, or *tsukaiyaku*. In the eighteenth century the *yōninza* (liaison office) was created, and the *yōnin* was subdivided into *soba-yōnin* (daimyo's personal stewards), *omote-yōnin* (administrative stewards), and *kattehō-yōnin* (financial stewards).

hama   A fishing village, interchangeable with *ura*, under the control of the *ofunateza* (office of the maritime magistracy) in the *kattehō* (finance department) of the *han*. *Hama* residents' corvée consisted of sailor duties for the *han*, in addition to *unjō* tax imposed upon their boats and fishing nets.

han   A daimyo's domain.

han-ura   Literally, "semi-fishing village." In contrast to the regular fishing village, residents of *han-ura* were bound to serve only one-half of their sailing obligations, but they were under the jurisdiction of the agricultural office and thus they carried out all the duties as peasants.

hikan   A retainer vis-á-vis the lord; during the Tokugawa period, it actually meant a servant of a samurai.

hinin   Both *hinin* and *eta* were outcastes, but whereas the *eta* status was hereditary, the *hinin* status was either hereditary or decreed. Although the *hinin*'s status was below the *eta*'s, a non-hereditary *hinin* was eligible to return to his original status. *Eta* were exclusively engaged in leather handicrafts, but *hinin* were engaged in providing popular entertainment, begging, and with tasks related to executions.

hitokerai   A townsman who acquired the status of a retainer of a samurai for the purpose of obtaining privileges in his business activities.

Honzan school   A Buddhist sect of mountain ascetics founded by Priest Zōyo of the Tendai sect.

hyakushō meshitsukai   A servant employed by a peasant.

ichimon   Same as *go-ichimon*.

Ikkō sect   The popular name for the Jōdo Shinshū sect of Buddhism, founded by Priest Shinran (1173–1262), which emphasized salvation by faith alone. During the Muromachi period it spread largely among the peasants. In the fifteenth and sixteenth centuries, *Ikkō* peasant believers frequently rose in rebellion against the ruling class. Also called *Shinshū*.

isshomochi   A holder of a private domain consisting of one district (*gō*). Some *isshomochi* did not actually hold one district but they all descended from members of the Shimazu daimyo's family. In social status, they were placed below *ichimon*, but there was no distinction between the thirty *isshomochi* and the thirteen *isshomochi*-equivalent.

isshomochi-kaku   *Isshomochi*-equivalent. See above.

jitō   The head of a district (*gō*) whose *gōshi* were like his own retainers and who actually came under his command in time of war. *Jitō* previously lived in the district of appointment, but during the early seventeenth century most of them were moved to Kagoshima. Councilors (*karō*) and other high-ranking officials held the post of *jitō* concurrently, without definite tenure.

joshi   A daughter or an unmarried woman in a household.

jūjitsu   Japanese martial art, from which modern *jūdō* developed.

kan   Same as *kammon*.

kammon   A unit of money equal to 1,000 *mon* copper.

kado   An administrative unit in the *kadowari* land allotment system. The *kado* was the tax-paying unit which usually consisted of the *myōzu* and several *nago* households. See *myōzu* and *nago*.

kengo   A kind of *hinin*.

kerai   A follower or attendant of a samurai.

koban   A castle-town samurai status, below the *yoriai-nami* and above *shimban*, created in 1706, of which there were 760 households. They were authorized to commute on horseback.

kogashira   A subunit chief.

kogumi   A subunit.

koku   A unit of measurement of grain equal to 4.9629 bushels.

koshōgumi   Same as *okoshōgumi*.

machi   A town. In Satsuma, there were only three communities which were accorded the legal status of *machi*. They were Kamimachi, Shimomachi, and Nishidamachi, all located within the castle-town of Kagoshima.

meshitsukai   A servant.

mon   A basic unit of money; a copper.

musume   A daughter.

myōzu   The head of a *kado*. Also see *kado*.

nago   A subordinate member of a *kado*.

naijo   Literally, "inner woman", denoting a female servant in a samurai household.

naishi   A priestess in the service of a Shinto shrine.

nanushi   Assistant village head elected from among *myōzu*.

ōbangashira   The head of an *ōbangumi* (outer guards), which was renamed *koshōgumi* or *okoshōgumi* in 1786.

ohanshita   One of the lower-ranking maids employed in the daimyo's grand chamber.

okoshōgumi   Outer guards. See *ōbangashira*.

otona   Village elders. In Satsuma it was a common name for *myōzu*.

otsugi   One of the middle-ranking maids employed in the daimyo's grand chamber. She served in the room next to the daimyo's.

rōnin   A samurai unattached to a lord. Also called *ukiyonin*.

sankin kōtai   A daimyo's alternating period of residence in Edo.

shimban   Literally, "new guards," a rank below *koban* and above *koshōgumi*, with stipend between 100 and 200 *koku*.

shōya   A village head appointed from among samurai, usually *gōshi*.

toshigyōji   Yearly supervisor. One each was elected from among the elders of the three towns of Kagoshima. He was charged with the general administrative duties of his town.

Tōzan school   A Buddhist sect of mountain ascetics founded by Priest Shōho of the Shingon sect.

tsukai-onna   A female servant.

uchi   A wife. Literally, "one who remains inside."

ukimen   A plot of rice paddy or dry field allotted to samurai for the purpose of providing their sustenance. In principle, *ukimen* could be sold and purchased. It was only lightly taxed and its owner was not subject to corvée duty.

ura   See *hama*.

ura-myōzu   A fishing villager privileged to own a *kako-yashiki* (a seaman's residential compound), which was also called *ura-*

yashiki (fishing village residence compound), in a fishing village.

yakunin   1. Lower-ranking officials. 2. The *yakunin* in private domains were equivalent to the *gōshi* elders in the other districts.

yashinaigo   A foster child who would not become an heir and whose adoption may or may not be legitimatized.

yokome   Inspector. His duties included the investigation of quarrels, criminal investigation, and the meting out of punishments. He was posted not only in districts but also at finance and harbor offices and at the *han* quarters in Edo.

yoriai   Lowest rank among the upper-class samurai. In 1712 nineteen households were *yoriai* and five were *yoriai-kaku* (*yoriai*-equivalent).

yoriai-nami   *Yoriai*-equivalent. See above.

yoriki   A quasi-samurai attached to various bureaus and offices such as kitchen, armory, navy, stable, falconry, etc.

yōshi   A person who is adopted as an heir.

宗門手札改條目

一 宗門手札改様之條々

切支丹宗門、就御大禁、前々より御領國中人數宗門手札被下置候、依之、此節、手札改被仰付候付、切支丹宗門幷一向宗改様之次第

1 切支丹宗門之儀、別テ入念遂穿鑿、若不審成者於有之八、早速搦捕之可申出候、且又、御領内御禁止之一向宗之儀、是又入念相改之、尤、右宗旨之者於有之八、可有披露事

2 一向宗之儀、寶永三年戌改巳後、頭取、本尊・書物・佛具持に相究候者、本人幷家内男女拾五歳以上之者、手札之肩書被仰付候付、宗門改役所より書付相渡候間、手札幷帳面、前一向宗と肩書可有之、當時同家内之者タりといふ共、右本尊等差出候以後入來候者八、肩書申附間敷候、尤、右同家内ニて前一向宗と肩書仕筈之者、當時別家内入候共不相替肩書可申附之、若又、右致肩書筈之者餘方に參候八八、其所改檢使互ニ問合之上、手札幷帳面、前一向宗と記置、双方改檢使罷

歸候節、宗門改役所ェ其屆可申出事

　但、同門徒之者も右同前書付相渡候間、此者共ハ一人躰一人に肩書可有之候、妻子等ハ肩書御免許候といへとも、右妻子之内ニモ一向宗志之者可有之候間、密々承究、不審之者於有之ハ、其旨宗門改役所ェ早々可申出候

3　先改、前一向宗と手札肩書有之者ハ、如其新札可記之事

4　依一向宗之咎百姓に申附置候もの共訴人等儀ニ付以前之姿御赦免之者、并先年一向宗相究肩書申附置候者其以後爲出後本尊・書物・佛具類差出候者共之儀、宗門改役所より書附相渡候間、如前々手札可出之、此者共ハ、前一向宗之肩書手札迄を御免候間、可有其心得候、尤、帳面ニは其旨委細可記置事

5　先年以來一向宗本尊・書物・佛具等致格護置、近年の一向宗改に親類或は下人或名子之者致所持之由ニて品々差出、其身ハ右宗旨ニて無之躰ニテ罷居者有之由候付、致沙汰可申出之段、延寶五巳年以來申渡候処、於に今右類之者有之由候条、不審成者於有之ハ入念致詮儀、彌以一向宗に相究候者ハ、早速宗門役所ェ可申出事

6　出家・山伏・神子・門長・兵道者・博士・其外取出類致祈念之砌、先祖拜來昔之
佛或一向宗阿彌陀之崇有之由密々申聞人を誑ニ付、一向宗志之者不致斷絕候、向
後右躰之者於有之ハ、當人ハ不及申與中之者に至迄、曲事可申附候条、此旨其所
之諸役人エ惱ニ可申渡候事

7　前一向宗と手札幷帳面ニ肩書之者、又ハ、手札片書御免ニテ帳面迄前一向宗肩書
之者、札改帳面を以相糺、別册相調、且又、右躰之者致死失候節ハ、宗門改役所
根帳消除事候間、右別册之奧に其旨相記、宗門改役所エ可差出事

二　御一門幷嶋津下總・嶋津若狹・嶋津圖書・嶋津豐前
其身獨禮幷大目付格以上・萬石以上改樣之事

1　島津周防殿・嶋津兵庫殿・嶋津讚岐殿・嶋津安藝殿・嶋津下總・嶋津若狹・嶋津
圖書・嶋津豐前右八人、其身夫婦嫡々夫婦、手札御免、雖爲隱居・後室、御免候

事

2　御子様、獨禮ニテ無之家ェ被爲入養子候得ハ、夫婦并養父母、手札御免候事

但、獨禮ニテ無之人ニテモ、妻

御子様ニテ候得ハ、緣與之內、夫婦共ニ手札御免、雖爲隱居又ハ後室、手札御免

3　御子様獨禮ニテ無之家ェ被爲入養子候節、御實母迄モ被召附候得ハ、右之御實母

手札御免候事

但、御女子様同斷ニ付御緣與之節も右同斷

4　御役ニ付獨禮之人、父母手札御免候事

但、御役御免以後ハ可爲手札

5　家格又ハ御役ニ付獨禮之人、其家妾腹之實母ハ可爲手札事

6　嶋津周防殿・島津兵庫殿・嶋津讚岐殿・嶋津安藝殿ニ男より末子迄息女方モ、家

内被罷居候内ハ手札御免候事

但、別立又ハ養子縁附之節ハ、其家格之通可被仰付候

7　御城代・御家老・御側詰・若年寄・大目附・大目付格ハ、御役ニ付テハ其身夫婦
手札御免、御役御免以後ハ可爲手札事、御一門幷獨禮之面々・御城代・御家老之
妻ハ、札改方帳面何某奧ト可書記事

8　萬斛以上之面々、其身夫婦嫡々夫婦隠居後室迄モ、手札被成御免候事

9　御一門方・御家老・一所持・一所持格・寄合・寄合格幷御側御用人・表御用人・
町奉行・御側役・御側役格迄ハ、宗門手札改帳内諸證文等迄も役人可致印形、其
外之面々ハ可爲直印形事

10　右何レモ直子出生候ハ、近所之士不及證判、宗門改帳書載、役人印形ニて可差出

之、尤、手札御免之衆ハ、御格之通可有之事

但、養子又ハ息女縁與互之出入、役人證文を以帳面可相究候

11 島津周防殿・嶋津讚岐殿・嶋津安藝殿・島津下總・嶋津若狹・嶋津圖書・嶋津豐
前、右家中士之儀ハ、手札無年附名字付可書記之、主人之縱名（假カ）不及肩書、家々一
所領地之郷を可書記候、召仕之女ハ內女と相記、手札年附可相除候、帳面ニ八家
中士幷內女共年附可相記之事

12 島津周防殿・嶋津兵庫殿・嶋津讚岐殿・島津安藝殿家來、別府・中村・肥後・新
納・曾木・日野・町田・川上・町田・近藤、栗川・矢野拾貳家、其身夫婦幷嫡子
夫婦迄ハ手札帳面共年附被成御免候、右之者共娘緣與之儀諸士同前被仰付、俗生
附迄モ被成御免候事

13 右四家家來梅元七右衞門・緒方喜三左衞門・中村三十郎・川上休右衞門・比志島
休左衞門・本田小源五・伊集院八兵衞・安山三左衞門・梅元平左衞門・樺山助左
衞門・詫間彥輔・浦川杢右衞門拾貳家之儀、延享三寅年依願前条之拾貳家差次之
格被仰付候間、手札帳面幷緣與等之儀可爲右同斷事

14 嶋津兵庫殿家中士之儀ハ、手札帳面共年附相除、主人假名不及肩書、一所之郷を

可書記、召仕之女ハ内女ト可書記候、且又、家中士娘幷内女札之者、諸士・諸組
與力・鄉士致緣與候節ハ、手札帳面共ニ年附相除俗生付迄を可相記旨、安永二巳
年依願被成御免候事

15 嶋津兵庫殿元祖加治木拜領之節諸士居附之盡三百七拾人餘被召附置候子孫之内、
御城下ヱ被召出、又ハ依譯斷絕等ニおよひ、當分之現家部三百拾七家、嫡々迄以
來三百拾七家之内何ノ何某と被仰付、右末家ハ此以前之通手札帳面無年附被仰
付、外家來之儀モ是又以前之通手札肩書なしニテ帳面年附被仰付候旨、文政三年
辰二月被仰渡候事

16 嶋津周防殿・嶋津讚岐殿・嶋津安藝殿・嶋津下總・嶋津若狹・嶋津圖書・嶋津豐
前家中士娘幷内女札之者、諸士・諸組與力・鄉士ヱ致緣與候節ハ、帳面迄年附い
タし、手札之面年附相除俗生付迄を可相記事

17 梶山邊路爲番人、嶋津豐前家來百拾三家内被召移置候處、遠方山中之故傍輩中之
娘入緣與無之候附、社家・寺門前・町・濱・在鄉之者共之娘、乍御法違、依願明

和五子年より先貳拾ケ年ツツ及三度縁與御免被仰付置候處、　年數筈合、　又々依願

嘉永元申年より先貳拾ケ年、　以前之通被成御免事

18　嶋津豊前ェ梶山在番所御預被仰付、　他領境目足輕勤方多候處、　人數差支候故、　都

城野町人足輕代召仕度、　境目郷町人同前名字付之願申出、　名頭計名字附被成御免

候事

19　御一門方以下一所持之足輕・座付中間等之娘、　士幷郷士・與カェ緣與屹と不相成

旨、　文政七年申七月被仰渡候事

20　肩書名字之儀

公義ハ勿論御國家ニてモ一向無之事ニテ不相幷候間、　向後一統被相止、　是まて肩

書之者又ハ末々迄モ都テ書下被仰付、　尤、　士緣與御免之差別有之儀ハ、　身分の以

格式先規之通卜仰付候、　且又、　書下相成候ニ付、　身分之格式迄モ相替候樣心得違

不都合之致方有之候者ハ、　無名字可被召成旨被仰渡候事

21 大崎之內菱田村ェ都城抱地有之、嶋津豐前家中士三拾五家內被居候之處、浦人同格之樣間々唱候儀有之、依願、都城菱田與卜手札被仰付候事

22 嶋津周防殿足輕家部別テ相少相當之緣與難調、依願天保十二丑年より先拾ヶ年重富諸在幷蒲生・東鄉・清水・志布志持切在之內百姓入緣與被成御免候處、嘉永三戌年迄ニテ年限筈合候事

23 嶋津若狹足輕家部別テ相少相當之緣與難調、依願天保十二丑年より先拾ヶ年華岡中浦・町幷諸在百姓入緣與被成御免候處、年限筈合、又々嘉永四亥年ヨリ先拾ヶ年是迄之通被成御免候事

24 種子嶋彈正殿事、別段之思召を以、一世御一門方次、島津若狹一列之頭被仰付候付、家來共手札面彈正殿一世家名方同樣被仰付候旨、弘化二年巳六月被仰渡候事

三　一所持より寄合並改様之事

1　一所持・一所持格・寄合・寄合並之面々妻ハ何某内と手札帳面共可相記之事

2　寄合並以上之面々、妾腹に嫡子致出生、其妾を實母札ニ願出候儀ハ札改間ニ申出、御免之人ハ御用人證文被出置候間、右證文見届實母札可出候、尤、手札帳面共年附可相除事

附可相除事

3　小番以下之面々實母札願之儀モ右同斷、御免之者ハ御勘定奉行證文被出置候間、右證文見届實母札可出候、尤、手札幷帳面とも年附俗生可相記事

4　以前より寄合並以上之面々妾年附有之實母札申請、又ハ小番以下之者妾手札年附相除實母札取來候者ハ、有來通にテ被差置候間、其通手札可爲取事

5　一所持・一所持格・寄合・寄合並之家中士、手札帳面共致年附名字附ニテ何某内

と可書記候、召仕之女ハ內女ト書記、尤、年附可相記候、從前々右之通記來事候
得共、手札ニ主人之名肩書有之帳面ニ主人之名不相記モ有之候間、一統相並候樣
可有之事

但、右之內、御城代・御家老幷其身獨禮之家中士ハ、手札肩書帳面迄モ何某殿
內と如先規主人之名ニ殿文字可相附候

6 島津要人足輕家部相少互之緣與難調、依願弘化二巳年より拾ケ年新城中浦人幷百
姓娘入緣與被成御免候事

四 御役格又ハ萬唱樣之事

1 寄合並以上之家格ニテ無之人大番頭・寺社奉行・御勘定奉行・御小姓與番頭・當
番頭御役相勤候人之家來ハ、手札帳面共致年附名字附ニテ何某內と可書記候、召
仕之女モ內女と可書記年附可相記候、御役御免以後タりといへ共屹御役爲相勤人

ニて候間、家来共名字附可為右斷事

但、右御役相勤候人一世之事候、至子孫ハ其家有来通可有之候

2 其身一代ニテモ小番ニテ御役ニ付テハ御鐵炮奉行以上無役ニテハ地頭職被仰付置候面々家来、手札年附いタし名字附ニて何某家来と可書記候、召遣之女ハ仕女と書記可致年附候、御役・地頭職御免以後ハ有来家格之通可書記事

3 諸御役人・諸士并以下之者共、妻と可書記事

4 達　貴聞縁與被成御免候諸士エハ、足輕・御口之者・御小人・御數寄屋仕坊主又ハ家中士名字附之者之娘・内女札之者縁與不被成御免候、乍然、本妻離別又ハ死後罷成右躰之者之娘内々ニテハ致妾置嫡子且又二男以下致出生候ハ、實母札可被成御免候、尤、御作事奉行以下諸御役人并二百石以上面々エモ以前之通右格式之者之娘縁與不被成御免事

但、實母札ニテモ不致本妻同前之筋、年附・親之名并何方座付・家中士等之譯手札帳面共ニ可相記候、親相果候ハ八兄弟又ハ家部之者之名可書記候

5 宗門手札改方帳面幷手札之面ニ、御一門を初・諸士幷以下之者娘又ハ召仕女、名之上ニオ之字附候テ書記間敷候、岡野・尾上・乙抔ト附候儀ハ不苦事

6 凡下者之娘、何某女子と認候モ有之候得共、以來ハ娘ト相認候方可相心得旨、寛政十二年申八月十九日、久馬殿より田畑武右衞門以御取次、無屹被仰渡候事

五　無格改様之事

1 龜山勇・山田諸三、無格被仰付候付、手札幷帳面本占方ニテ相改、札面札改奉行所と相記、檢使之儀ハ御家老與檢使兼務被仰付候、家來之儀ハ手札帳面共年附名字附ニテ何某家來と相記、召仕之女ハ年附ニテ仕女と可相記旨、天明六年午正月被仰渡候事

六　出家・山伏幷格式相替社人改様之事

1　出家・山伏成、寺社奉行所可爲證文事

但、當山派山伏ハ修驗宗、本山派山伏ハ天台宗と、手札之面宗旨付可有之候

2　南泉院・福昌寺・大乘院・淨光明寺・坊津一乘院・國分彌勒院・大龍寺、右七ヶ

寺現住、年頭御禮之節ハ着座之僧候故、手札御免、隱居ハ可爲手札事

3　千眼寺着座之門首座順、一乘院ニ被仰付候旨、天保八年酉十一月被仰渡候事

4　壽國寺着座之門首、大龍寺次ニ被仰付候旨、文化十一年亥九月被仰渡候事

5　不斷光院着座之門首席順、福昌寺次ニ被仰付候旨、文化十四年丑九月被仰渡候事

6　志布志大慈寺事、現住紫衣之僧住職之節ハ着座被仰付候付、手札御免、着座無之

住持ハ可爲手札事

7　着座之門首ハ他國僧ニテモ御格之通手札御免、帳面ニモ御免之譯可記置事

8　達　貴聞住職被仰付候寺院ハ、其門首之證文にテ可相改之事

但、出家之儀ハ都テ不及年附候

9　他國出家御當國寺持ハ御國僧同前之事候、寺持外ニテモ御國居付御免之僧ハ、其身より願不申出候ても、向後不洩樣手札可相渡候、尤、何國之出家師匠何僧之由門首證文ニ寺社奉行添書を以手札相渡之、右之譯幷宗旨附手札帳面共ニ可記置事

但、右之僧他國ェ出候ハ、其宗旨改僧より出人帳面ニ書載檢使ェ差出、手札可取揚候

10　遍歷之出家ハ、手札改之節其宗旨改僧より出人帳面書記檢使ェ差出古札可取揚之、歸國候テ新札取候ハ其門首之可爲證文事

11　飯限山蓮光院事寺格大乘院次被仰付、以來出世平僧之無差別着座門首被仰付候旨、

文政十一年子正月被仰渡、以後願出趣有之、家督迄手札御免被仰付候旨、天保二

年卯五月被仰渡候事

12 飯隈山蓮光院家より別立梅谷坊・櫻井坊・十寶坊・松尾坊・榎木坊・池

之坊・杉谷坊右八坊之儀八都テ家内俗躰之者共迄救仁郷名字被成御免候間、手札

帳面共ニ名字可相記候、且又、右坊中沙門之儀八平日之唱書附等八家號用間敷事

但、蓮光院事家筋モ相替候付、家來名字附被成御免候

13 飯隈山蓮光院家來娘縁與之儀、寄合家來娘縁與同樣被仰付候旨、文政七年申七月

被仰渡候事

但、内女之儀モ寄合内女同樣被仰渡候

14 飯隈山蓮光院家來之儀、以來救仁郷蓮光院内と片書可相記旨、文政七年申九月被

仰渡候事

15 國分正宮八幡一社幷衆徒ママ・殿守、八幡・新田宮社人之儀、名字附來候者八、以前之

通名字附無年附士互之縁與被成御免候事

但、披官附之者、先改之通、神前手次と手札帳面ニ可書記候

16 穎娃開聞社人、紀・長山・愛甲・榊・宇都宮・上野・井上・丸田・長倉・松山十

家之者共、以前之通名字附無年附、士互之縁與被成御免候事

17 當所諏訪社之儀　御崇敬格別之神社候間、被召附置候候三拾家部之社家、此節御取

譯を以嫡子迄無年附被仰付、不及願縁與取組候士又ハ郷士・與力ニハ手札帳年

附俗生附ニテ縁與被成御免、二男以下ハ是迄之通被召置候旨、文政七年申十一月

被仰渡候事

18 鹿兒嶋琉球寺光明寺并諸所居住之琉僧之儀、札元不相除、修學ノたメ大和エ罷登

之由候故、當所にテ手札之不及沙汰事

19 高山四拾九所大明神社家古來より貳拾四家部有之候處、近年及困窮相當之縁與難

叶無妻者のミにテ往々社家斷絶仕外無之候間、當年より先貳拾ヶ年郷内町・在・

寺門前互之縁與御免被仰付被下度旨申出、願之通寛政十一_未年より及兩度被成御

免候處、年限筈合、又々依願天保十亥年より先キ貳拾ケ年以前之通被成御免候事

20本田出羽守并井上駿河守事、着座門首格式被仰付、願出趣有之、家督迄手札御免

被仰付候旨弘化二年巳五月被仰渡置候事

21般若院着座門首席順飯限山蓮光院次ニ被仰付候旨弘化四年未二月被仰渡、以後願

出趣有之、家督迄手札御免被仰付候旨嘉永四年亥十一月被仰渡候事

七　大奥女中一巻改様之事

1大奥ェ御奉公に罷出候女中、士并人家來・町・濱・在郷・寺門前之者にテモ、手

札御廣敷役所ェ格護いタし置、札改之節札改奉行所ェ差出、御奉公中ハ可爲無札

事

但、御暇被下候節ハ御廣敷御用人證文可出候

2 右同斷首尾宜敷方にテ御暇被下候女中之儀、御次以上相勤候者ハ、人家來幷町・濱・在郷・寺門前之者タりといへ共士緣附御免之事候間、御暇被下候砌、於參先新札申請候様ニと御廣敷御用人より證文可出事

但、俗生附、不及年附候、御牛下相勤候者ハ、首尾能御暇被下候テモ、士緣附不被成御免候

3 首尾不宜方ニテ御暇被下候女中、人家來幷町・濱・在郷・寺門前之者、士ニ緣付可相障候、手札之儀ハ、出本札主方新札申請候様ニと御廣敷御用人より證文可出候、士娘之儀ハ、其節之沙汰次第可申附之事

4 輕身分ニテ大奧御次以上相勤首尾能御暇被下候者ハ、士・郷士エ緣與被成御免儀候付、本之俗生ニハ不被召歸、士格式之者家內ニ可被入置候間、御暇被下候節御廣敷御用人より右之趣其身共エ時々申聞、家元之儀夫々手便を以相賴願出候様被仰付候、自然家元難賴得者、右成行御廣敷御用人より得差圖候様被仰付候旨、文化十二亥六月被仰渡候事

八　小番幷新番・御小姓與改樣之事

1　代々小番相勤候者之子共、幼雅(ガ)有之御番不相勤內ハ、家來共下人と可書記候、御
番相勤候節ハ御格之通家來名字可相記事

2　小番之者ェ八鄉養子御免不被仰付事候得共、無是非願出候者ハ御小姓與ェ被召入
御格ニ候間、家格被相下候節ハ家來共下人札可申請事

3　諸人男女共ニ古札帳面見合、相違於無之ハ如先規手札可出之事
但、名字有之者ハ同姓と不相記、末子迄銘々名字可相記候

4　士生子ハ直子無別条旨鹿兒島八近所之士兩人證文、鄉八五人與、五人與無之所ハ
近所之鄉士兩人證文を以、新札可出之事

5　別立・養子成又ハ緣與其家內相除人ハ、互之證文を以手札可相直事

6
嫡子相果候歟又ハ養子ニ遣候節、二男を嫡子ニ成願申出右ニ準三男以下男上リ相願、二男以下右同断之節モ依願男上リ御免被仰付儀候得共、向後嫡子相果又ハ養子ニ遣候節嫡子成願之儀ハ只今迄之通ニテ三男以下男上リ不被仰付候、然なから右之内御支族又ハ為差立家筋ニテ二男三男エ男上リ有之候得ハ家格・進上物等宜相成候家柄之面々ハ是迄之通男上リ願申出、家格・進上物等にモ不相掛家筋ハ嫡子成之外男上リ願不及申出生之形ニテ被差置、家格・進上物等ニ不相懸嫡子養子違變ニテ立歸者ハ本家之長子ニ被入置、以後別立をも願出候節ハ諸事其家之二男之格式ニ被仰付候、尤、男上リ之儀前条之通被仰付置候間、二男以下養子違變ニテ立歸候者ハおのツカら本之次第ニ入來筈候、嫡子以下進上物等格式宜者養子ニ遣候跡男上リ致居違變ニテ立歸候者、本之姿ニハ不被仰付其家之末子同様之格式ニテ本家之家内ニ被入置候、別立願出候ハ諸事其家之末子同様之格式被仰付候、乍然、二男三男エ男上リ無之者ハ違變以後ニ二男又ハ三男之場ニ被仰付候旨、安永八年亥四月被仰渡候事

但、郷士之儀モ右同前相心得、首尾方之儀ハ先格之通可致候

7
嫡子相果又ハ養子ニ遣候節二男を嫡子ニ相願候得ハ、依家柄三男以下男上リ願出

來候得共、其通ニテハ二男以下幾人も有之候筋ニ相成候付、以來ハ生之儘ニテ二

男より末子ニ至迄男上リハ不被仰付候、依之たとへハ二男

御目見不仕以前相果候得ハ、三男ハ三男之形ニテ

御目見被仰付、進上物等も三男之通可被仰付候、尤、何男ニテモ嫡子相願候儀ハ

有來通、寬政十一年未四月被仰渡候事

8　養子成爲致家督者之家內ニテ手札申請候養父母之子共ハ、養姉妹養何と都テ養之

字可書記事

但、養父母致養ひ子置候ハ、養父何某養ひ子何と可書記候

9　不達　貴聞緣組取與候士幷諸組與力・鄕士エハ足輕・御口之者・御小人・御數寄

屋仕坊主又ハ家中士、名字附之者之娘・內女札之者緣與被成御免候得共、此跡之

通之妻札ニハ不被仰付候、妻札ニテ年附、妻之親之名幷何方座附・家中等之譯手

札帳面等書記可申候、親相果候ハ、兄弟又ハ家部之モのの名ヲ可書記事

但、內女ニテモ此跡之札改ニ手札帳面ニモ不書載者、內女ニ召仕候由ニテ除證

文有之候共、本文之通ニハ不仰付候

10 小番・新番、妾腹ニ出生いタし候子ハ、其身書物・近所之士両人之證文・大番頭座より當人宛之添書を以札改奉行所エ申出、免許證文ニテ直子札可申受事

11 御小姓與右同斷之節ハ、其身書物・近所士両人之證文・小組頭次書・御小姓組番頭奥書を以可爲右同斷候事

12 諸與與力同斷之節ハ、其身書物・近所士両人之證文ニテ御兵具方ハ肝煎、御廣敷ハ小頭、夫々次書、支配頭奥書を以右同斷たるへき事

但、郷士永代下女腹ニ出生之子直子札願出節ハ、其身書物ニ五人與并組頭・郷士年寄次書、地頭奥書を以可申出候

13 諸士家内札ニテ罷居候者娘、士筋惱成者ニテ候者、不達　貴聞縁與取組候者エハ被成御免候事

14 士家内札又ハ足輕・御口之者・御小人家内札之者ニテモ名字附有之、足輕・御口之者・御小人・御數寄屋仕坊主同格之者ニテ筋目惱成者之娘ハ、不達　貴聞縁與

仕候者ニハ被成御免候事

　但、右躰無名字者之娘ハ士エ縁與不被成御免候、併、右腹ニ士之子共致出生候

一八、吟味次第實母札ニハ可被成御免候

15　社家・寺門前者之娘、士エ縁與不被成御免事

16　社家・寺門前・町・濱浦人・百姓之娘、依譯士幷郷士エ縁與御免ニテ元文二巳改
　以前ニ妻札申受置候者共不及年附候、妻親之名前幷何方社家・寺門前・町・浦濱
　人・百姓等之譯手札帳面共ニ可書記候、親相果候ハ、兄弟又ハ當分家部之者之名・
　俗生可書記事

17　右同斷之者娘、士妻札申受置、夫相果當分祖母又ハ實母札ニテ罷居候者、右同斷

18　右同斷之者娘、部屋栖之者ニ致縁與妻札申受置、子共無之內夫相果、直ニ其家之
　養ひ娘抔ニいタし置候者、右同斷

一九　右同斷之者、改以後致緣與未妻札不申受者ハ、俗生相紀御勘定奉行證文被出置候
間、證文見屆右同斷相改手札可爲取事

二〇　右同斷之者娘致妾置、子共致出生實母札申受置候者も、都テ右ニ準手札可相渡事

二一　士并郷士エ、下々之者娘緣與又ハ右之子共致養子儀、御禁止之事候間、能々入念
可相改事

二二　郷士鹿兒嶋士被召成候者之妻子ハ、古札見合相違之儀無之候ハ、同前手札可相直
候、父母之儀其家內入手札願候者ハ、本在所之郷士年寄役々證文ニテ手札可出之、
札之面何某家內札父母之譯肩書可有之候、其外兄弟親類家內札之者共ハ、本之在
所ニテ手札可相渡事

二三　士ニ被召出候者之妻子手札相直候儀、右同斷、父母右家內札願出候者、鹿兒島ハ
其支配頭、郷士郷士年寄役々、私領家中者ハ有來候格式之證文ニテ手札如願可出
之、尤、手札之面帳面迄も父母之譯可相記之、父母不被召出候者ハ札之面前々之

之姿ニテ手札可相渡事

姿ニ可相記之、其外兄弟親類家內札之者共ハ士札爲取候儀堅御禁止之事候間、前

24 親類又ハ妻之列子等無據者、新規ニ士之家內入手札願候ハ、其子細書記、親類
幷近所之證文、夫々支配頭次書を以、札改奉行所エ申出可相究事

　但、鄕ハ親類・近所・五人組證文鄕士年寄次書地頭奧書、　私領ハ有來書物を以、
札改奉行所エ申出相究事候間、　先改何方何某家內ニテ何樣札取候譯、古帳見届
帳面ニ其旨相記、　改濟候節別冊書拔可差出候

25 士・鄕士幷凡下之者娘、　親依科鄕士之下女被仰付置候者之腹ニ出生之子有之候ハ、
手札取方等之儀札改奉行所エ申出可相究事

26 諸士手札紛失・虫附・燒失・疵付等之節、　筋々之次書・奧書を以申出來候得共、
向後ハ其身書物直ニ札改所エ差出、　夫々支配頭エハ屆迄を可申出候、尤、直子札・
實母札願ハ有來通可有之事

　但、鄕士之儀モ右同斷、其身書物・五人組・横目・與頭・鄕士年寄次書を以、

札改所ェ可申出候、尤、地頭ェ八屆迄を可申出候

27 士幷郷士御暇申出家中入候者八、以來共歸參候儀御禁止之条、若永代致暇候節八、親類之家內相附札を爲取、手札帳面本何某親類ト肩書可相記、尤、名字相除年附可有之事

28 士幷郷士之妻致離別女子母方ニ付遣候娘立歸候家內ニテ介抱難成、或右外ニテモ家內罷居候女子、或離別之實母後之夫相果右式介抱難成又八無據譯ニ付、脇方家內ニテ可致介抱候間何某何と手札被仰付度旨家內替之願申出候八、吟味之上由緒於無別条八願之通手札可爲取事

九 諸組與力幷足輕類・諸役座付者改樣之事

1 一代諸組與力被召出候節八、御用人以證文手札相渡、一代與力之譯手札帳面共可

相記之事

2　右同斷之者、本家內人數其身家內ニテ手札申受度旨申出候ハ、支配頭證文ニテ家內入差免、手札帳面共本之姿ニテ手札爲取、以後家部元相果候節ハ、本々之通手札相直候儀紛敷無之樣可相改事

3　右被召出候以後其身緣與之儀、諸士御免不被仰付格之者ニテモ本妻ニ致候儀、不苦候、然共俗生之儀可相記事

4　右同斷之節、妻ニ取與又ハ出生之子共之儀、其身相果候ハ、本足輕家督家內ニテ手札可爲取事

但、右娘之儀、達　貴聞緣與取組之者エハ、御免無之候

5　足輕・御口之者・御小人・御數寄屋仕坊主手札帳面共、名字附年附可相記事

6　足輕・御小人・御口之者・御數寄屋仕坊主手札出入ハ、支配頭可爲證文事

7 右妻・娘・下女・下人等手札相直候儀ハ、其座之肝煎可爲證文事

8 足輕・御小人・御口之者・御數寄屋仕坊主之儀、下女札之者ニテモ妻札可相直節

一、支配頭證文ニテ可相究事

9 諸役座付者共、手札帳面共ニ名字附ニテ致年附、足輕以下互之縁與御免之事

10 右同斷座付之内ニも人足躰之者ハ、無名字何方之者ニテも養子・縁與等取與之儀、不苦候事

11 諸座附之儀、士幷郷士・與力ェ縁與不被仰付旨、文政七年申六月被仰渡候事

12 御駕籠之者・御挾箱持・御食焚數年首尾能相勤候者ハ、御見合之上、其身計名字

附御免之事

十　郷士幷諸所締方之郷士改様之事

1　郷士高帳家部之外、札改帳面別家部ニ立間敷候、高奉行所エ毎年相納候郷士高帳家部之通、無相違様可相調事

2　郷士直子有之者、致養子儀御禁止候、然といへとも直子定病・片輪者抔ニテ其家相続難成譯有之者ハ、其段申出、地頭承届候上、養子差免事候間、右躰之者入念相改手札可出之事

3　郷士他所エ居住之者、本在所ニテ手札可相渡候、家内幾人憖ニ手札申受候旨、本在所之證文を取、居住之在所ニテ改檢使エ可差出事

4　郷士之娘、諸家中又社家・寺門前類年附有之家内ニ致縁與候者ハ、其家内同前手札年附可相記之事

5 諸郷ェ罷居候浪人并大村郷足輕之子共、其郷郷士ェ互之致縁與妻札ニ申受候儀御
免ニテ候、其郷より他郷ェ致縁與儀御免無之候事

　但、下女・下人外之郷ェ出入之儀ハ御構無之候

6 甑嶋之儀ハ一嶋ニテ地方ニ相替入來者も無之、郷士相當之縁與難調候付、嶋中百
姓・浦濱・社家類互之縁與御免候間、所役人證文ニテ手札可相直事

　但、年附・俗生附等之儀ハ、御格之通可相記候

7 志布志郷士新地并川原田・昆沙ケ野・大河內邊路番人共、山中故致縁與者無之候
付、町人・百姓・社家・寺門前者之娘緣與被成御免候、尤、餘例ニハ不被仰付候
事

　但、年附・俗生付等之儀ハ、御格之通可相記候

8 志布志田之浦之內ニ本松ェ邊路番所被召建、番人貳人引移定番被仰付候付、右番
人之儀ハ、町人・百姓・社家・寺門前者緣與安永八亥年被成御免候事

　但、年附・俗生附等之儀ハ、御格之通可相記候

9　高岡・倉岡・綾・穆佐四ヶ所之儀、女少場所ニテ郷士共相當之縁與不相調、其上
逼迫者共ニテ、内場郷より掛テ之縁與猶以難成、諸事差支自血筋致斷絶ニ付、日
雇ニ召置候女共腹ェ出生之子、乍御法違直子札之願申出跡々御免之事候得共、元
文五申年御法違之儀候故、自今以後不被成御免段被仰渡置候、然共右之通女少場
之儀候故、町人・百姓之娘縁與之願申出候ハハ御吟味之上被成御免儀も可有之旨
被仰渡置候間、右御免之者ハ、地頭證文之上、出生之子直子札ニ可爲取事

但、右之妻致離別候ハ、其届札改奉行所、間ニハ御勘定所ェ申出、以後同様之
縁與取組候節ハ、是又同前届可申出候、尤、年附・俗生附等之儀ハ御格之通可
相記候

10　野尻之内紙屋村之儀他領境目ニテ、缺落者之節俄人數召寄候儀度々有之候故、郷
士人數漸々相減候テハ御用之支相成筈ニ候、然處山中之在所殊極貧者共ニテ傍輩
中之縁與不相調無妻而已ニテ罷居候付、依願野尻幷小林中百姓・野町人之娘縁與
被成御縁候、尤、餘例ニハ不被仰付事

但、年附・俗生附等之儀ハ御格之通可相記候

11 小林郷士木浦木番人之儀ハ、麓より遠方之山中ニテ傍輩中之娘縁與不相叶、右場
所他領境目ニテ譯も相替候付、願之上以來共所中町人・百姓之娘縁與御免候事
但、右通縁與御免ニテ候處、又々依願寶暦九卯年須木・加久藤、町・在郷者之
娘縁與被成御免候、尤、年附・俗生附等之儀ハ御格之通可相記候

12 一代郷士被召出候以後、其身縁與諸士御免不被仰付格之者ニテモ本妻ニ致候儀不
苦候、然共俗生附ハ可相記事

13 佐多邊塚居住郷士、麓より四五里程相隔山中殊ニ逼迫者共ニテ、所中ハ勿論他郷
より縁與不相調、願之趣有之文政七申年ヨリ先拾ケ年百姓娘入縁與被仰付置候處、
天保四巳年迄年限筈合候事

14 預り郷士之儀何某家エ被召附置候譯、帳面等エ無之候テハ至後年紛敷儀も可有之
候間、以來手札帳面迄右書ニ其譯相記候様、文政七年申十二月被仰渡候事

15 高岡郷士籾木平右衞門・二見休右衞門事、定番幷去川關所相堅候以御取譯、下人

共百姓娘緣與被成御免候事

十一　諸家中幷諸士下人改樣之事

1　小番家中名字附之者娘、且又諸士下人札之者娘ハ、諸士妻札ニハ都テ不被成御免候、乍然妾ニいタし置子共致出生候節ハ、吟味次第實母札可被成御免候事

但、鄉士之儀も右同斷

2　家中者名字附之儀、或書下、或片書格式之通記來事候得共、都テ書下被仰付候間、其通可書記之、無名字之者も主人ヨリ名字差免候ハ、其家中同前名字可相記候、且又名字附御免無之家中入候者、其家中同前名字可相除事

3　家來・下女・下人出入ハ互之以證文可相究事

4　諸縣郡　高城四ケ村ェ、北郷作左衞門家來ェ黑木喜太郎・二見金藏・黑木源五郎・永
　　峯瀨助・二見金五郎・二見半助・永峯七左衞門・二見甚右衞門・井上半右衞門・
　　永峯五郎左衞門・井上仲兵衞致居住罷居、邊路締方等之譯ニ付、依願野町・在郷
　　者之娘緣與被成御免候事

5　代々小番相勤候者之家來、手札致年附名字附ニテ何某家來と可書記候、召仕之女
　　下女と可書記候、一代小番・代々新番相勤候者ハ、家來名字附御免之事
　　但、家來之内鄕ェ致居住其所ニテ手札取來候者も可有之候間、相違無之樣可致候

6　御小姓與相勤候者之内、先祖共御役幷地頭職又ハ家筋之由緖無構、家來之儀ハ名
　　字相除下人ト可書記事
　　但、家來鄕居住之者モ右同斷

7　諸士召仕之者ェ、無名字ニテ家來・披官と手札記來候者も、下人と可書記事

8　大河平休四郎飯野ェ在番役ニテ被差置候處、依願家來共、百姓幷野町之者緣與御

免之事

9　飯野境目在番大河平六郎兵衞下人、邊鄙之場所ニテ無妻之者而已有之、依願野町
者幷百姓互之縁與被仰付旨、享和元酉七月被仰渡候事

10　陪臣召仕之者ハ都テ下人札ニ可申付事

11　士中エ、百姓・町・浦濱人・社家・寺門前者之娘、支配頭以證文年季抱置候内、
何方之者エ取合候共、出生之子ハ抱主人方エ可相附事

但、夫婦者以免證文年季抱置候内子共出生候ハ抱主人エ可相附候、夫婦者之內
夫を年季抱置候妻ハ本在所エ差置子共出生候者ハ、其子母方エ可相附候、妻を年
季抱置夫ハ本在所エ罷居、若右之妻本夫之子共爲致出生候儀有之候者、抱主人
エ可相附候、且又抱主人エ被附下候子共之父百姓・町人・浦濱・社家・寺門前
者ニテ候ハ、其子下人札可申附候、又ハ父諸士家來札之者名字付之者ニテ候ハ、
出生之子ハ父同前名字附可相記候、乍然抱主人之下人名字付御免無之格之人ニ
テ候者、尤可爲無名字候、夫を年附抱置下女ニ取合子共致出生候ハ、出生之子

右ニ可相準候

十二 社人・内侍・地神・平家座頭幷寺門前者改様之事

1 福ケ迫諏訪神主井上大和守代致上京、吉田家ェ神道葬祭之作法致傳授候付、以來
神職相勤候者迄手札帳面共ニ神職と相記、家内之者ハ以前之通宗旨附被仰付候旨、
享和元年酉五月被仰渡候事

2 社家、神職被仰付候者ハ、寺社奉行以證文可相改之事

3 当所社家之娘縁與等、又ハ下人・下女出入證文之儀ハ、支配頭次證文を以可相除
之事

4 社人之儀ハ一統手札之面名字附年附可相記候、士縁與ハ不被成御免候事

5 社家・寺門前者餘方ェ永代手札相除候儀ハ寺社奉行所可爲證文事

6 右之者共娘縁與、又ハ下人・下女等相除候節ハ、先規之通以證文可相究事

7 百姓社家、神職被仰付候者、又ハ別立候者、當所諏訪神主以證文可相改之事

8 寺社家召仕之者無名字之者ハ、下人と可書記候、披官・家來又ハ内と書記間敷事

9 當所内侍之儀、俗生無構社役相勤候内迄、手札帳面共年附ニテ何某何と致肩書、當所守社家改可相附候、尤、内侍職断申出免許候ハ、相當之縁與可爲勝手次第事

寺
當所守社家改可相附候、

10 始羅郡　山田陽春院門前者共、及困窮相當之縁與不相調、所中野町・百姓弁帖佐・加治木・溝邊・蒲生野町・百姓・人家來互之縁與文化十二亥年以來年限を以被仰付置候處、年限筈合、又々天保八酉年ヨリ先拾ケ年是迄之通御免被仰付置候處、弘化三午年まてニテ年限筈合候事

11　郷・私領内侍之儀、郷士幷家來其外末々之者ニテモ其身依願一節兼務內侍職相勤
　事候間、社人之妻外之內侍ハ手札改方其俗生次第相片付、社役相勤候內ハ何方何
　宮内侍と手札帳面共ニ片書迄を可記置候、尤、夫持之內侍社役相勤候內出生之子
　ニモ夫之家內ニテ手札可爲取候、且、未致緣附內內侍ニ罷成其後緣與取與之儀不
　苦候間、出生之子手札前条可爲同斷事

12　地神・盲僧・平家座頭ハ、都テ俗生相紛手札帳面共可記置候、子共之儀ハ親俗生
　之通片付手札可爲取事

13　南泉院門前者之儀、手札幷帳面ニモ何屋と家名可書記事

14　諸寺院門前者、　先規之通可爲無名字事
　但、福昌寺役人之儀ハ先規之通名字附、　大乘院・淨光明寺・大龍寺・興國寺・
　南林寺・妙谷寺、　右六ヶ寺役人之儀ハ、　有來通手札帳面共年附名字附可相記候

15　福昌寺役人三家之儀與入不被仰付候間、御小姓與等之內より養子罷成者無之、今

通ニテハ家致断絶外無之候付、三家共此節與入被仰付被下度旨願被申出趣有之候

得共、其通被仰付候テハ、古來より被召附置候御趣意致相違由緒モ薄方相成趣候

条、願通ニハ難被仰付候、併致家断絶候テハ猶以被召附置候詮不相立候条、御取

分を以右三家之儀、御格式無構郷士又ハ諸組與力之内ヨリ養子成、寛政八辰四月

被成御免候事

16　寺門前者男女共、諸士之家來幷諸座付之者ェ致縁與手札不相直者ハ借銀利銭仕日

雇之方相見得候間、出生之子ハ門前ニ相附、双方ェ科銭壹貫文宛可申附之事

但、　科銭申附以後、^{候脱カ}　縁與無別条旨申出候共取揚間鋪候

17　寺門前幷社人札改帳、別册可相調事

18　高岡・綾・倉岡・穆佐社人之儀、同社家中之縁與難成、依願四ヶ所百姓・町人之

娘縁與御免被仰付候間、時々願可相立候、尤、不縁又ハ別立テ右同断縁與之節ハ、

是又同前可申出之事

19 福昌寺門前者之内、西郷・妬良・飯牟禮・松元・佐藤・前田・圖師・宮里・染川・
西田・鮫嶋・山之内・鈴木・東・種子田・兩大山・池田・宮原・松下・永田貳拾
壹家之儀ハ、由緒之依譯、嫡子又ハ隱居迄名字附御免之事

20 加久藤社人同所二之宮現王頭取黒木多中、同所社家中、此以前ハ七家有之候得共
當分四家ニ相成、其内三家無妻ニテ罷居、所中又ハ近郷ニ至リ相當之縁與不相調、
今通ニテハ往々社家斷絶いタス外無之候間、加久藤・小林・飯野百姓・野町人之
娘縁與、依願天明元丑年被成御免候事

21 高原挾野權現丼右同所東御在所社家依願郷内丼小林・高崎百姓野町人入縁與、寛
政十二年申年以來度々年限を以被仰付置候處、年數筈合、又々天保八酉年ヨリ先
貳拾ケ年郷内丼高崎・小林、野町・在郷・寺門前互之縁與被仰付候事

22 高原神德院丼右同所錫杖院門前者、依願所中ハ勿論高崎・小林百姓野町人縁組、
寛政十二申年以來度々年限を以御免被仰付置候處、年數筈合、又候天保八酉年よ
り先キ貳拾ケ年、以前之通被成御免候事

23　帖佐心嶽寺門前者、小身者共ニテ遠方相掛緣與不相調、無是非永代暇申出漸々致
衰微當分男女纔計罷居、今通ニテ八近年斷絕可仕儀御座候付、百姓・町・浦人・
家來之類互之緣與御免被仰付被下度願申出趣有之、町・浦人幷家來互之緣與天明
六年七月一往被成御免候事

24　帖佐願成寺門前者漸々及減少候ニ付、依願町・濱人幷家來一往緣與被成御免候旨、
明和六年丑十二月被仰渡候事

25　帖佐心嶽寺下人、邊鄙之場所ニテ同格之者有少、依願百姓・町・浦人・家來之類
互之緣與一往被成御免候旨、　丑十二月被仰渡候事

26　財部佛性院門前者八、元來小身者共ニテ近年猶又困窮仕、他鄕ェ相掛相當之緣與
不相調無妻者而已有之、漸々人數及減少、依願所中百姓・野町互之緣與天保二年
卯四月より先拾ケ年被成御免候處、天保十一子年迄ニテ年限筈合候事

27　鹿兒島郡吉田津友寺門前者共少人數ニテ無妻者而已故、所中幷他鄕百姓互之緣與

之願申出趣有之、度々年限ヲ以御免被仰付置候處、年限筈合、又々依願弘化二巳

年ヨリ先キ貳拾ケ年以前之通被成御免候事

28 高岡法華嶽寺門前者共、少人數罷成相當之緣與不相調、依願天保四巳年ヨリ先貳

拾ケ年郷士下人・野町・百姓共互之緣與被成御免候事

野町人互之緣與被成御免候事

29 川邊寶福寺門前者并下人、脱躰勞者共ニテ相當之緣與難調、依願天保十亥年ヨリ

先貳拾ケ年、所中并谷山・知覽・加世田・川邊郡 山田・阿多・田布施・伊作百姓

野町人互之緣與被成御免候事

30 同所玉泉寺門前者共、脱躰勞者ニテ相當之緣與難調、依願天保十亥年ヨリ先キ貳

拾ケ年、所中并谷山・知覽・加世田・川邊郡 山田・阿多・田布施・伊作百姓野町

人互之緣與被成御免候事

十三　苗代川者一巻改様之事

1　苗代川之者共、氏當分拾七姓迄之由候、依之名之上面々氏を一字宛可書記候、勿
論名字ニて八無之候、格式モ此中之姿ニ候、且又、李達馬・伸十圓・朴春盆・伸
春松事八先年伊集院郷士格ニ被仰渡候、右四人之者共嫡子迄を郷士之格ニ被召成、
二男ヨリ八此中之通ニ可差置候、氏之字被成御免候儀八、本國ニテ持合之字候故、
二男ヨリ八此中之通ニ可差置候、氏之字被成御免候儀八、本國ニテ持合之字候故、

一字宛氏之字書候儀被成御免候事

2　苗代川ェ百姓・浦濱・町其外之女入縁與八被成御免候、苗代川之者脇方ェ縁與出
候儀堅御禁止之事

但、大奥ニテ御次以上之御奉公相勤首尾能御暇之女八、御差圖次第何方ェモ縁
與可被成御免候、尤、其節八御廣敷御用人證文之上手札可相渡候

3　李達馬・伸十圓・朴春盆・伸春松四家之者共、養子・縁與之儀同格中互之致取組
筈候得共、人數少相當之取組難叶候八、苗代川中由緒之者ェ八養子・縁與可被成

御免候事

4　鹿屋笠野原ェ被召移候苗代川者、互之縁與出入等之儀、前条同斷相心得改方可有
之事

5　朴泰潤事、數十年朝鮮通事相勤候御取譯を以、嫡々迄伊集院郷士格被仰付候旨、
文政五年午十月被仰渡候事

十四　鹿兒嶋町人改樣之事

1　鹿兒島上・下・西田町、縁與・養子等ニ付テ、右三町外浦濱ェ出候者ハ、町奉行
可爲證文事

但、下女・下人他方ェ相除候儀ハ、前々之通可有之候

2　右同斷ニ付三町中ェ互之出入ハ、年行司・五人組可爲證文事

3　三町之內、同町中同斷之出入ハ、五人與可爲證文事

4　鹿兒島上・下・西田町之者、緣與・養子成等ニ付テ浦濱エ相除、又ハ浦濱エ右次ヨリカ
第鹿兒嶋三町エ入來候者ハ、町奉行所・御舟手エ申出、兩奉行以證文札元可相除
事

但、右三町且又兩御舩手附之者并南泉院・南林寺・志布志大慈寺・同大姓院・
同海德寺・同永泰寺門前之儀ハ、水主ニ相立候ニ付、町・浦濱互之緣與御免ニ
テ候、其外浦濱役不相勤者ハ右緣與御免無之候

5　鹿兒島町人、名頭計都テ名字附御免候間、家部之者迄手札帳面共名字可相記事

6　三町ハ勿論諸郷等之無差別、差上金致候御取譯を以被召出候者ハ、以來都テ嫡々
迄家內入被仰付候旨、文政十年亥十月被仰渡候事

十五　百姓幷野町人改様之事

1　諸士・家來幷寺門前・社家召仕之下女、在郷ヱ入縁與ハ御免ニテ候間、主人以證
文所役人より郡方ヱ申出、郡奉行證文ニテ百姓妻札可相直事

但、右之通縁與御免ニテ候處、嫁罷居妻札不相直者、借銀利錢仕日雇之方ニ相
見得候、依之双方ヱ科錢壹貫文宛申附、出生之子ハ在郷ニテ手札可爲取候、右
躰之者縁與無別条旨申出候共取揚間敷候

2　諸士幷社家・寺門前者召仕之下女、致日雇置候百姓ヱ取合子共致出生候ハ、其
父百姓家内ニテ手札可爲取候、尤、御法違之故、御法之通双方ヱ科錢壹貫文宛可
申付之事

3　諸士之家來幷諸座付・社家・寺門前者在郷ヱ入來候者ハ、郡方ヱ申出、郡奉行以
證文百姓手札可爲取事

但、士幷郷其外何方者ニテモ百姓方ヱ賣渡郡奉行證文有之者ハ、手札不申請內

ニテモ、又々本之通抱先相替間敷候

4　右同断之者、百姓下人・下女被下候節ハ、郡奉行以證文下人・下女札可申請候、

尤、札元より被下先ェ手札除方之證文、格式之通可有之候、右手札見届、新札可相渡候事

但、郷士下女之儀ハ郷士召仕、百姓下人・下女之儀ハ百姓召仕ト名目被相替候旨、文政元年寅五月末川將監御取次を以被仰渡置候間、郷士永代抱者之儀ハ是迄之通下人下女ト相認、依科郷士百姓ェ被下候者迄、以來手札帳面共ニ召仕ト可相記候

5　百姓之子不依男女百姓共養ひ子ニ致候者并百姓妻列子之儀も、郡方ェ申出、郡奉行證文ニテ札元可相除之事

6　百姓家内を差分候儀ハ、檢地門割又ハ家内人數多罷成候節、郡奉行見計之上爲別立儀候間、札改ニ付、名頭又ハ名子附等之儀不書違、古帳引合、先改以後別立候者ハ郡奉行證文之通可書記事

七、郡奉行承候上百姓養子仕置候者且又嫡子ヱ名頭相譲候儀ハ、郡見廻・庄屋證文ニ
テ札改之節名頭可相直候、嫡子・養子外ヱ相譲候者ハ、郡方ヱ申出郡奉行證文ニ
テ名頭可相究候事

　但、名子出入等之儀、郡方ヱ申出、郡奉行證文ニテ可相究候

八、門地致附屬候者ハ、先名頭何左衞門・當名頭何左衞門、且又跡地方受取候者ハ、
當名頭何左衞門・先名頭何左衞門と、手札帳面共ニ可相記之事

　但、百姓共男子、都テ一字名相付候テハ男女紛敷候付、相付間敷候

九、百姓之內定病幷片輪者之肩書有之者ハ、其人柄見屆手札可相渡候、若肩書相送之[違カ]
者ハ、急度可申出之事

十、社家・寺門前者娘幷下女・下人、在鄕・浦濱ヱ入緣與ハ御免之事候間、致緣與候
者ハ百姓幷浦濱ヱ手札可相直之事

　但、右通緣與御免ニテ候處妻札不相直召置候者ハ、借銀利錢仕日雇之方ニ相見
得候間、双方ヱ科錢壹貫文宛申付、出生之子ハ在鄕・浦濱ニテ手札可爲取候、

縁與無別条旨訴申出候共取揚間鋪候

11　百姓社家、　自分官名附間敷事

12　百姓男女共餘方ヱ出候儀御禁止候、然といへとも年季に出候者ハ、郡奉行證文ニ
テ鹿兒嶋士相抱候儀ハ御免許候、尤、札元相直儀ニテハ無之事

13　百姓又ハ野町之者縁與ハ、庄屋・部當・郡見廻以證文手札可相直事
但、縁與ニ付別郷ヱ相除候節ハ、郷ハ郷士年寄、私領ハ役人以證文可相除候、
百姓ヱ野町ヨリ入來儀ハ御免ニテ候、百姓より野町ヱ出候儀、且又野町ヨリ町・
浦濱類ヱ互之出入御禁止候

14　百姓弁野町ヱ脇々より縁與又ハ何そニ付入來候者、離別又ハ子細有之本在所ヱ相
除候節ハ、郡奉行證文たるへキ事
但、出生之子ハ郡奉行以證文父方ニテ手札可申請候

15　野町之者より百姓共ヱ入縁與ハ御免之事候間、百姓妻札可爲取候、且又嫁罷居百

姓妻札不相直者ハ、借銀利錢仕日雇之方ニ相見得候間、双方ェ科錢壹貫文宛可申

附候、縁與無別条旨申出候共取揚間敷事

16 依科郷士幷百姓、召仕之格を以私領預リ被仰付候者ハ、惣テ於預先手札申受候様、

弘化二年巳四月被仰渡候事

17 横井野町之儀、御上下之節御泊御休場所ニテ、御供宿等無支様無之候テ不叶儀候

處、勞所ニテ妻求候儀不相調候付、横井野町と百姓互之縁與被成御免候間、郡奉

行免以證文可致縁與事

（ママ）

18 高岡・綾・穆佐・倉岡野町人之儀、百姓共互之縁與御免之事候、尤、郡奉行免證

文を以可致縁與候、證文無之者又ハ内場之百姓ェ縁與曾テ仕間敷候、且又右四ヶ

所郷士下人之娘町中之者ェ縁與御免之事候、町人共之娘郷士下人方ェ遣候儀ハ御

禁止候事

19 高岡・綾・倉岡・穆佐野町人名頭幷子共・伯父・甥・從弟類迄、名字付御免候事

20諸縣郡吉田野町者ェ、依願百姓之娘緣與御免之事

但、郡奉行證文有來通可有之候

21飯野・加久藤・小林五日町十日町野町人共、名頭計名字附御免候事

22野尻野町人之儀、紙屋御番所付ニテ御用之咨人有之候節御番所より召仕事候處ニ、
近年致困窮相當之緣與不相調往々町人相減御用差支筈候付、依願野尻幷小林中百
姓之娘緣與被成御免候、尤、餘例ニ八不被仰付候事

23吉松野町之儀求摩通路飛脚宿等其外眞幸表奉公人止宿之場所ニテ候處、近年段々
勞入、本拾六家內ニテ候得共八家內ニ相成、皆無妻ニテ不町立、往々御用難勤躰
相成候ニ付、依願百姓互之緣與被成御免候事

24大口野町之者共連々致困窮、餘郷野町より入緣與無之無妻之者而已ニテ、近年人
數相減諸奉公方難勤、今躰ニテ八往々不町立筈候間、百姓入緣與御免被仰付度旨
願申出候處、諸奉公方難勤、殊他領境目之儀候故、寶曆四戌年願之通被成御免候

事

25 高崎野町之者共、人少所、殊逼迫者共ニテ他所より爲縁與入來者無之、依願寶暦
五亥年百姓縁與被成御免候處、又々依願所郷土下女縁與被仰付候旨天保九年戌四
月被仰渡候事

26 高尾野町之者共、前々より至極致困窮、諸殿役百姓同前相勤、難町立譯を以、依
願寶暦七丑年百姓縁與被成御免候事

27 山野野町之者共致困窮、他郷遠方エ相掛致縁與候儀不相調、依願寶暦八寅年百姓
互之縁與幷人家來・下人より入縁與被成御免候事

28 栗野野町之者共勞入他方エ相掛緣與不相調、依願寶暦八寅年所中百姓互之縁與被
成御免候事

29 鶴田野町之者共勞入、近年猶以致困窮御奉公方相勤者も無之、依願寶暦九卯年所

中百姓縁與被成御免候事

但、本文之通御免被仰付置候處、又々依願文政七申年より天保四巳年迄拾ケ年

近郷百姓互之縁與被仰付置候處、年限筈合、又候依願天保九戌年ヨリ先拾ケ年

所中弁佐志・宮之城・大村百姓互之縁與御免被仰付置候處、弘化四午年迄ニテ

年限筈合候事

30 踊野町之者共勞入相當之縁與難調、依願寶曆十一巳年以來所中弁近郷百姓互之縁

與等年限を以御免被仰付置候處、年限筈合、又々天保八酉年ヨリ先貳拾ケ年所中

弁近郷百姓互之縁與被成御免候事

31 他國者、居付手札申受野町ェ被差置候者共、諸所野町・百姓共ェ縁與出入、庄屋・

部當・郡見廻可爲證文事

32 浮免百姓弁移百姓等、郡奉行可爲證文事

33 百姓共ェ先年被下置候他國者男女共ニ手札出入、郡奉行可爲證文事

但、年季座不及證文候

34 百姓之下人・下女他郷百姓ヱ相除節ハ、双方郷士年寄・郡見廻以證文札元可相除
候、且又其郷中ヱ相除候節ハ、郡見廻・庄屋證文まてニテ札元可相除候事

35 百姓之下女百姓ヱ嫁候者、郡見廻・庄屋以證文、札改之節、百姓妻札可相直事

36 諸郷野町幷浦濱人之儀ハ、百姓・浦人同前之者ニテ候故、名字附御免無之候、然
共境目郷之儀ハ依願名頭計名字附御免之事

37 小林五日町十日町両野町、勞者共ニテ相當之緣與不相調無妻者而已有之、所中ハ
勿論近郷社家・寺門前・百姓之嫁入緣與之願申出、願之通當年より先年數拾五ケ
年御免被仰付候旨文化十二年亥三月被仰渡置候處、年限筈合、又々依願文政十三
寅年より先拾五ケ年以前之通御免被仰付置候處、年限筈合、又々弘化二巳年より
先拾五ケ年以前之通被成御免候事

38 曾木野町之儀、纔少人數ニテ相當之緣與不相調、依願百姓互之緣與、文化十二亥年以來及兩度年數拾ケ年宛御免被仰付置候處、年限筈合、弘化二巳年より先キ拾ケ年以前之通被成御免候事

39 穎娃野町之儀、相勞相當之緣與難調、依願文化十二亥年以來、所中幷知覽・鹿籠・川邊・河邊郡山田・喜入・今和泉・指宿・山川浦濱人・百姓互之緣與、年限を以度々被仰付置候處、年限筈合、又々天保八酉年より先貳拾ケ年以前之通被成御免候事

40 姤羅郡山田野町之者共、相勞相當之緣與難調、依願文化十二亥年以來年限を以、所中百姓幷鄕士下人、溝邊・加治木・帖佐・重留百姓互之緣與被仰付置候處、年限筈合、又々天保八酉年より先拾ケ年以前之通御免被仰付置候處、弘化三午年迄ニテ年限筈合候事

41 大崎野町之者共、相勞相當之緣與不相調、依願明和四亥年より大崎・志布志百姓入緣與被成御免候處、又々依願文政七申年より拾ケ年串良百姓互之緣與被仰付置

候得共、年限筈合、又候天保八酉年より先キ拾ケ年是迄之通被仰付置候處、弘化

三午年迄ニテ年限筈合候事

42 市來城之町野町及困窮互之縁與調兼、依願明和四亥年より市來諸在入縁與被成御

兔候處、又々依願天保九戌年より先キ拾ケ年、串木野・伊集院・日置・吉利・永

吉・伊作・田布施・阿多百姓互之縁與御兔被仰付置候處、弘化四未年まてニテ年

限筈合候事

43 野尻野町人及困窮、依願明和五子年、所中并高崎・高原・小林百姓縁與被成御兔

候事

44 串良野町及困窮、依願明和六丑年ヨリ貳拾ケ年、所中并高山・大崎百姓入縁與御

兔被仰付置候得共、天明八申年迄年數筈合、其後御兔無之候處、又々依願寛政五

丑年より先貳拾ケ年完度々御兔被仰付置候處、年限筈合、又々天保五午年午より

先貳拾ケ年以前之通被仰付候事

45　高山野町人相勞、依願明和七寅年以來度々年限を以所中百姓幷波見浦より入緣與

被仰付置候得共、年限筈合、又々寬政十二申年より串良唐仁町浦幷波見浦互之緣

與度々被仰付置候處、年限筈合、又々來子年ヨリ先キ貳拾ケ年以前之通被成御免

候旨、嘉永四年亥二月被仰渡候事

46　羽月野町、極々逼迫者共ニテ相當之緣與調兼、依願明和七寅年ヨリ貳拾ケ年所中

幷山野・大口・曾木百姓入緣與御免被仰付置候得共、天明九酉年迄年限筈合、又

々依願所中幷近鄕山野・大口・馬越・曾木右四ケ所百姓入緣與寬政十一未年より

先キ貳拾ケ年被成御免候處、文政十五寅年迄年限筈合、又々依願文政六未年ヨリ

先貳拾ケ年所中幷山野・大口・馬越・本城・曾木百姓入緣與、天保十三寅年迄ニテ

年限筈合、又々依願嘉永元申年ヨリ先貳拾ケ年菱刈中百姓入緣與被成御免候事

化カ

47　高岡八代南俣村・北俣村、右兩村女少場所ニテ百姓無妻之者餘多有之、耕作仕附

方等も存之儘ニモ不相成候付、依願明和七寅年ヨリ佐土原御領內百姓娘入緣與被

成御免候、宗旨證文等不紛樣致置、其節々願可申出事

48 高岡深年村女少場所ニテ、右同斷依願寬政八辰十月ヨリ佐土原御領內百姓娘入緣
與被成御免、尤、宗旨證文等無紛樣致置、其節々願可申出事

49 末吉野町、勞者共ニテ他所ヨリ爲緣與入來者無之、依願明和四年亥三月ヨリ所中
百姓互之緣與被成御免候事

50 今和泉野町勞者共ニテ相當之緣與調兼、明和二酉年以來所中ハ勿論近鄉百姓・浦
人互之緣與年限を以及度々御免被仰付置候處、年限筈合、又々天保八酉年より先
拾ケ年所中幷喜入・指宿・頴娃百姓・浦人互之緣與御免被仰付置候處、年限筈合、
又々依願弘化四未年ヨリ先貳拾ケ年喜入・指宿・頴娃・谷山・山川・知覽・鹿籠・
坊泊百姓・浦濱・野町互之緣與被成御免候事

51 恒吉野町、勞者共ニテ相當之緣與調兼、漸々人數相減候ニ付、依願明和四亥年九
月ヨリ所中百姓娘緣與被成御免候事

52 松山野町及困窮、依願明和九辰年以來拾五ケ年宛及度々所中百姓互之緣與被成御

免候處、年限筈合、又々依願天保八酉年ヨリ先拾五年以前之通被仰付候事

53　大村野町人勞者共ニテ相當之縁與不相調、依願明和九辰年以來度々年限を以所中近郷百姓互之縁與被仰付置候處、年數筈合、文政八酉年より拾ヶ年宮之城・佐志・山崎百姓互之縁與被仰付置候得共、年限筈合、又々天保九戌年より拾ヶ年所中幷宮之城・山崎・藺牟田・佐志・黑木百姓互之縁與被仰付置候處、年限筈合、又々嘉永四亥年より先拾ヶ年是迄之通御免被成候事

54　伊集院野町勞者共ニテ相當之縁與難成候付、依願明和九年辰五月より先キ拾ヶ年所中百姓互之縁與被成御免候處、年限筈合、依願所中幷近郷百姓互之縁與天明五巳年より被成御免候事

55　溝邊野町勞入相當之縁與不相調、依願明和九年辰五月より先拾五ヶ年所中百姓互之縁與被成御免候處年限筈合、又々依願所中百姓幷姶羅郡山田・加治木・日當山・横川百姓互之縁與天明六午年より拾ヶ年宛及度々御免被仰付置候處、年限筈合、又々天保八酉年ヨリ先拾ヶ年以前之通御免被仰付置候處、弘化三午年迄ニテ年限

筈合候事

56牛根百姓勞者共ニテ相當之緣與調兼、依願明和九年辰五月以來及度々年限を以所中百姓・浦人互之緣與御免被仰付置候處、年限筈合、又々依願天保三辰年ヨリ先拾五ヶ年以前之通被成御免候事

57鹿兒嶋郡吉田野町人及困窮、依願寶曆十三未年以前所中幷他鄉百姓互之緣與及度々年限を以御免被仰付置候處、年限筈合、又々依願天保八酉年ヨリ先貳拾ヶ年以前之通被仰付候事

58財部野町、依願明和元申年、都城・末吉・福山エ相掛百姓入緣與、被成御免候事

59財部野町萬次郎・亡龜次郎、當御時節柄ニ付同所北俣村之內部壹杉場エ差立置候杉六千本餘差上度申出、願之通被仰付、兩人共ニ亡父代ヨリ引續度々極難之者共相救其節々品物等被下置、其上辰年御借入銀被仰渡候節モ錢百五拾貫文完差上候付、諸奉公方拾ヶ年宛御免爲被仰付置者共ニテ、又候此節右通部壹杉差上度願出、

別テ奇特成心入之者共ニテ候間、旁之御取譯を以、両人共ニ一世名字附・山差帶候儀被成御免候旨、文化九年申三月被仰渡候事

60　國分兩野町、年行司相勤候者之家筋幷乙名之者迄、名字附被成御免候旨、天明五年巳正月被仰渡候事

61　國分本町・唐仁町之儀、由緒之以御取譯、屋敷持ニテ別立候者迄名頭成・名字附御免、屋敷讓渡無屋鋪相成候得ハ無名字被召成旨、文政七年申六月被仰渡候事

62　國分小村町之儀、依願由緒之御取譯を以、年行司首尾能相勤候者退役後幷名頭家督之者迄、名字附被成御免旨、文政十三年寅五月被仰渡候事

63　高原野町少人數ニテ相當之緣與不相調、依願高原中百姓緣與安永十丑年ヨリ先貳拾ヶ年御免被仰付置候處、當年迄年數筈合、依願來酉年ヨリ先貳拾ヶ年所中幷近郷諸在・寺門前者入緣與被成御免候旨寬政十二年申三月被仰渡候處、文政三辰年迄年限筈合候處、又々依願文政七申年ヨリ先貳拾ヶ年以前之通被成御免候處、天

保十四卯年迄ニテ年限筈合、又々依願弘化三午年より先貳拾ケ年郷内幷近郷社家・

守門前・百姓互之縁與被成御免候事

64 須木野町之者共少人數ニテ互之縁與不相調、所中百姓入縁與依願安永八亥正月
以來貳拾ケ年完及度々被仰付置候處、年限筈合、又々天保八酉年ヨリ先貳拾ケ年
以前之通被仰付候事

65 諸縣郡 高城之領境目ニテ、野町之者共ヤワラ捕方等致出精、諸所ヨリ召捕差
出候科人一宿之節下番申附繩差替等いタさせ、且、聞合彼是御用ニ付近地領ェ召
列差越候節無名字ニテハ不都合之儀而已有之候付、所横目共より訴申出趣有之、
天明五巳年願之通名頭迄名字附被成御免候事

66 陽之尾野町少人數ニテ互之縁與難調、依願所中幷近郷百姓入縁與年數貳拾ケ年安
永七年戌年以來度々以年限御免被仰付置候處、年限筈合、又々依願弘化二巳年ヨ
リ先キ貳拾ケ年是迄之通被成御免候事

67　蒲生野町労者共ニテ互之縁與難調、依願所郷士下人幷諸百姓互之縁與年數拾五ヶ年天明二年寅七月御免被仰付置候處、年限筈合、度々依願此節又々以前之通年數拾五ヶ年被成御免候旨文政十三年寅十一月被仰渡候處、弘化元辰年迄ニテ年限筈合、又々依願弘化三年年ヨリ先拾五ヶ年以前之通被成御免候事

68　國分兩野町、互之縁與迄ニテハ調兼、依願町・濱・寺門前・諸在エ相掛縁與、天明六午年ヨリ拾ヶ年完及度々御免被仰付置候處、年限筈合、又々依願弘化四未年ヨリ先拾ヶ年、所中ハ勿論、鹿兒島三町・重留・帖佐・加治木・敷根・福山・牛根・垂水・志布志・清水・曾於郡・日當山・横川・都城・財部エ相掛、町・濱・寺門前・郷士下人・諸在互之縁與被成御免候事

69　末吉野町人岩崎仁右衞門・加藤貞右衞門・岡崎傳右衞門・橋口次助・加藤次助・橋口善兵衞・橋口傳右衞門・加藤五郎右衞門・加藤與太郎・加藤次郎兵衞・加藤
^宛
傳右衞門・岡崎平次郎・宮田太右衞門・岡崎平助跡・岩崎仁助・橋口善助跡・岩崎利右衞門・加藤傳四郎・宮田喜兵衞・橋口善左衞門・猪俣善助・加藤萬助・岩崎善六・宮田太吉・岩崎源左衞門・岩崎仁太郎・橋口小太郎・橋口兼太郎、右貳

拾八人依願名字附被成御免候旨、天明六年午七月被仰渡候事

70　末吉野町岩崎源太郎・加藤萬右衞門・岩崎宇右衞門、右三人依願名字附被成御免候旨、寬政十二年申五月被仰渡候事

71　川邊野町、依願所中井川邊郡山田・知覽・阿多百姓互之緣與、安永五年申七月よリ先貳拾ケ年御免被仰付置候處、寬政八年辰七月迄年限筈合、其以後御免無之、又々依願寬政十一年未三月より先貳拾ケ年、所中井阿多・加世田・知覽・川邊郡山田百姓互之緣與、及兩度被成御免候處、年限筈合、又々依願天保十亥年ヨリ先キ貳拾ケ年、所中井阿多・加世田・穎娃・川邊郡山田・谷山百姓・浦人・下人・寺門前者互之緣與被成御免候事

72　華岡古江浦野町、家內人數繰計罷在互之緣與難調、依願所中町・浦・在鄉互之緣與當年ヨリ先貳拾ケ年被成御免候旨、文化二年丑二月被仰渡候處、年限筈合、又々依願所中町・浦・在鄉幷近鄉之內垂水・新城・鹿屋・大姶良百姓互之緣與、文政八酉年ヨリ先拾ケ年御免被仰付置候處、年限筈合、又々天保六未年ヨリ先拾ケ

年、以前之通御免被仰付置候處、弘化元辰年迄ニテ年限筈合候事

73　山崎野町之儀、脱躰逼迫者共ニテ相當之縁與調兼、文化十二亥年以來年限を以、所中ハ勿論、近郷社家・門前・百姓入縁與、度々被仰付置候處、年限筈合、又候弘化四未年ヨリ先拾ヶ年、是迄之通被仰付候事

74　高城郡高城野町之者共相勞、相當之縁與不相調、依願百姓互之縁與、寛政十二申年ヨリ先拾ヶ年完、及度々被仰付置候處、年數筈合、又候天保八酉年ヨリ先キ拾ケ年、以前之通御免被仰付置候處、弘化三午年迄ニテ年限筈合候事

75　知覽野町之者共相勞、依願所中幷近郷之內喜入・穎娃・鹿籠・山田・川邊郡百姓互之縁與、寛政十二申二月ヨリ先拾ヶ年完、及度々被仰成御免候處、年限筈合、又々依願天保八酉年より先拾ヶ年、以前之通御免被仰付置候處、弘化三午年迄ニテ年限筈合候事

76　横川野町及困窮、相當之縁與不相調、所中ハ勿論、近郷百姓又ハ山ヶ野金山御國

居附根帳付之者互之縁與、寛政十二年申三月以來、及度々年限を以御免被仰付置
候處、天保十亥年迄ニテ年限筈合候事

77 樋脇野町勞者共ニテ、依願所中并入來・山崎・東鄉百姓互之縁與、文化十二亥年
以來年限を以御免被仰付置候處、年限筈合、又候天保八酉年ヨリ先拾ケ年、是迄
之通御免被仰付置候處、弘化三年年迄ニテ年限筈合候事

78 馬關田野町咸少いタし、相當之縁與調兼、文政六未年より拾ケ年年限を以、所中
百姓互之縁與被仰付置候處、天保三辰年迄ニテ年限筈合、又々依願天保九戌年よ
り拾ケ年、以前之通御免被仰付置候處、弘化四未年迄ニテ年限筈合候事

79 野田野町人相勞、依願文政七申年ヨリ先拾ケ年、所中百姓互之縁與被仰付置候得
共、天保四巳年迄年限筈候事

80 出水麓町及困窮、餘鄉野町より入縁與相少無妻之者而已ニテ、依願阿久根町・水
引大小路町・限之城向田町男女縁與一往被成御免候旨、文政八年酉九月被仰渡候

事

81 鹿屋野町困窮者ニテ相當之縁與不相調、依願天保九戌年より先拾ヶ年、所中ハ勿論、鹿兒嶋三町人幷高隈・串良・高山・姑良・大姑良・大根占・花岡・新城・垂水浦濱人百姓互之縁與御免被仰付置候處、弘化四未年ニテ年限筈合候事

82 姑良野町勞者共ニテ相當之縁與不相調、依願嘉永元申年ヨリ先貳拾ヶ年、高山・串良・内之浦・大崎・志布志・鹿屋・花岡・新城・垂水浦濱野町ェ相掛、互之縁與・養子出入被成御免候事

83 東郷野町勞者共ニテ相當之縁與不相調、依願弘化二巳年ヨリ先拾ヶ年、所中百姓・浦町互之縁與被成御免候事

十六　御舩手附并浦濱人改樣之事

1　嶋津左膳領分帖佐之內松原浦并鹽屋在及困窮、其上脇元浦重留內ニ被召成公役等
相重候故、往々人數相減候テ八難勤譯を以、浦・在互之緣與年限を以御免被仰付
置候處、年限筈合、又々依願天明七未年ヨリ先貳拾ケ年、以前之通被成御免候處、
年限筈合、又々依願文化五辰年ヨリ先貳拾ケ年、以前之通被成御免候處、年限筈
合、又々依願當年より先貳拾ケ年、是迄之通被成御免候旨、天保二年卯二月被仰
渡置候處、嘉永三戌年迄ニテ年限筈合候事

2　兩御舩手附定船頭之者八、手札帳面共年附いタし名字付可相記候、尤、定水主以
下之者共無名字ニテ致帶刀來候得共、以來名字付被仰付候旨、文政八年酉五月被
仰渡候事

3　諸士之家來并社家・寺門前八、浦濱人エ入緣與八御免ニテ候得共、浦濱人エ內々
取合子共致出生候者、子浦濱ニテ手札可爲取候、內々取合候儀八御法樣違之事候

条、双方ェ科錢壹貫文完可申附之事

但、浦濱人之娘幷浦濱人召仕之下女、一先諸士幷人家來・社家・寺門前者之下
人共取合子共致出生候ハ、浦濱ニテ手札可爲取候、右準科物可申附候

4　諸士召仕之男女且又人家來・社家・寺門前者召仕之下人・下女等、浦濱ェ入緣與
致候儀ハ御免ニテ候間、入緣與之譯主人幷支配頭證文見屆、於無口能者ハ、浦濱
ニテ浦濱役人以證文手札可爲取候、御舩手ェ不及申出候事

但、右通緣與御免ニテ候處、妻札不相直召仕置候者ハ、借銀利錢仕日雇之方相
見得候間、双方ェ科錢壹貫文ッヽ申附、出生之子ハ浦濱ニテ手札可爲取候、緣
與無別条旨訴申出候共、取揚間鋪候

5　御舩手附之者餘方ェ出候ハ、御舩奉行可爲證文候、御舩手附之內互之出入ハ、御
舩頭可爲證文事

6　浦濱人緣與ニ付他浦之出入、御舩奉行可爲證文事

7　其所浦中之緣與ハ、浦濱役人可爲證文事

8 浦濱人名頭幷名字讓候者、且又家內差分別立候者ハ、御舩手エ申出、御舩奉行證文を以可相究之事

9 浦濱人之子共男女共ニ浦濱人養ひ子いタし候者、又ハ妻列子之儀ハ、御舩手エ申出、御舩奉行證文を以養ひ子ニ可相究之事

10 浦濱人召仕之下女を浦濱人妻札相直候儀ハ、御舩手エ不及申出候間、浦濱役人證文を以妻札可相直之事

11 浦濱人召仕之下女・下人、鹿兒嶋幷他鄉エ相除候節ハ、其鄉より御舩手エ申出、御舩奉行證文を以札元可相除候、其浦中エ相除候節ハ、御舩手エ不及申出、浦濱役人證文を以札元可相除之事

12 谷山松崎町四元名字一家之者共、由緒之譯ニ付、依願手札帳面共名字附被成御免候事

13　谷山松崎町・平川浦・和田濱三ヶ浦之儀脱躰勞浦之上、近年人少罷成相當之緣與

不相調、依願天保十五辰年ヨリ先拾ヶ年、所中幷近鄕百姓・家來・下人等互之緣

與被成御免候旨被仰渡候事

14　浦町濱町之儀、浦人濱人同格之者候間、改方之次第浦濱可爲右同斷事

15　御舩手附之者、　上・下・西田町互之緣與御免之事

16　浦濱町人定病幷片輪者之肩書有之者ハ、　其人柄見屆手札可相渡候、若肩書相違之

者ハ急度可申出事

17　串良唐人町浦之儀、別テ致困窮漸々人數致減少、緣與トシテ入來候者無之、依願

寶曆十辰年串良野町者入緣與被成御免候事

18　串良唐仁町浦之儀、　前文之通緣與御免被仰付置候處、　依願近鄕野町幷所中百姓互

之緣與、　寬政八辰年ヨリ先拾ヶ年完御免被仰付置候處、　年限筈合、又々天保七申

年より拾ケ年、以前之通御免被仰付置候處、弘化二巳年迄ニテ年限筈合候事

19 鹿屋北・南高須浦勞者共ニテ、他浦ェ相掛傍輩中之縁與不相調無妻而巳罷居候付、所百姓幷近郷最寄之百姓・新濱・野町等之內より互之縁與、當年より先拾ケ年御免被仰付候旨、天保二卯二月被仰渡候處、年限筈合、又々依願天保十二巳年ヨリ先拾ケ年、以前之通御免被仰付置候處、嘉永三戌年まてニテ年限筈合候事

20 垂水浦人、近年差迫リ他浦より縁與調兼、依願明和六丑年ヨリ貳拾ケ年ッツ及度々所中百姓互之縁與御免被仰付置候處、年限筈合、又々依願天保五年午年より先貳拾ケ年、以前之通被成御免候事

21 垂水柊原浦之儀、諸書附等ニ八柊原浦ト相認、札面ニ八柊原濱ト書載爲來由候得共、以來札面共柊原浦ト可相記旨天保十四卯閏九月被仰渡候事

22 喜入浦人及困窮、依願明和九辰年より先貳拾ケ年完、度々所中百姓互之縁與御免被仰付置候處、年限筈合、又々來子年より先貳拾ケ年、以前之通御免被仰付置候

旨カ
處、嘉永四年亥十月被仰渡候事

23 福山浦町之亡兵右衞門・亡彌兵衞事、櫻嶋燃ニ付助勢米等差出別テ志宜候ニ付、
　代々嫡子迄名字付被成御免、鹿兒嶋町人同前被仰付候旨、天明六年午正月被仰渡
候事

24 内之浦町之亡須田儀兵衞事、浦中ヱ合力米等差出候御取譯を以、代々名字附御免
被仰付候事

25 小根占大川浦少人數ニテ、依願所中百姓互之縁與、天明二寅年より先貳拾ケ年ツ
ツ、及度々御免被仰付置候處、年限筈合、又々依願天保十四卯年より先三拾ケ年、
以前之通被成御免候事

26 東郷白濱浦、右同斷依願所野町幷百姓互之縁與、年數拾五ケ年、天明七年未八月
より被成御免候處、享和二年戌七月迄年限筈合、又々依願文政六未年より先貳拾
ケ年被成御免候處、天保十三寅年迄ニテ年限筈合候事

二七　出水米之津町漸々相勞人數相減候付、依願當年より先貳拾ケ年、所中百姓・野町
人互之緣與被成御免候旨、寛政十二申三月被仰渡候處、文政二卯年迄年限筈合、
又々依願文政六未年ヨリ先貳拾ケ年、以前之通被成御免候處、天保十三寅年迄ニ
テ年限筈合候事

二八　指宿湊浦之亡濱崎太平次・右同所摺之濱之吉崎彌右衛門事、兼テ奇特成心掛之者
共ニテ、其上指宿
御光越之節段々御用之儀共有之候處宜相働、旁御取譯を以、代々名字附寛政六年
寅二月御免被仰付置候段、同十二年申四月被仰渡候間、末子迄モ名字附可相記事

二九　小根占町濱之儀及困窮、依願所中百姓より入緣與、年數貳拾ケ年完、寛政十二
申年より及兩度被成御免候處、年數筈合、又々依願天保十一子年より先貳拾ケ年、
以前之通被成御免候事

三〇　帖佐納屋町半浦ニテ候處、勞者共少人數ニテ相當之緣與不相調漸々人數致減少候
付、帖佐之內納屋町野町者ハ勿論帖佐十日町半浦・松原浦・鹽屋在迄互之緣與之

願申出、願之通文化十二亥年ヨリ及両度年限を以被成御免候處、年限筈合、又々

弘化二巳年より先キ拾ケ年以前之通被成御免候事

31 志布志町人共之儀、屋敷持家督之者迄名頭ト相唱名字相用候儀是迄之通、屋敷持

ニテ當時無名字之者モ右同様名字附可相用、町役之儀ハ勤中計名字附御免、其外

名頭之唱又ハ由緒モ不相知名字附來候者モ、以來名字相用候儀不相成旨、文化十

二年亥二月被仰渡候事

32 帖佐十日町之儀、半方半浦成御免被仰付置候處、此節又々依願都テ半浦成、他浦

縁與迄モ被成御免候旨、文化十二年亥三月被仰渡候事

33 大崎菱田浦相勞、依願文化十二亥年ヨリ拾ケ年、所野町幷所中野百姓互之縁與被仰

付置候處、年限筈合、文政八酉年ヨリ先拾ケ年、所中野町人・百姓入縁與被仰付

置候得共、年限筈合、又々天保八酉年ヨリ先拾ケ年是迄之通被仰付置候處、弘化

三午年迄ニテ年限筈合候事

34 吉利浦人相當之縁與不相調、所中百姓互之縁與、年數貳拾ヶ年、寛政十二年申五月御免被仰付置候處、文政二卯年迄年限筈合候事

35 谷山松崎町亡是枝助右衞門・是枝助十郎事、御時節柄を汲請差上銀致候御取譯を以、一世名字附被仰付候處、冥加御禮として此節金子差上、再往奇特成心入ニ付、代々名字附文化十五年寅正月被仰付候事

36 今和泉高目浦・瀬崎浦、依願野町ヨリ入縁與御免被仰付置候處、年限筈合、又々依願所中百姓・野町迄互之縁與、文政九戌年ヨリ先キ及度々年限を以御免被仰付置候處、年限筈合、又々依願弘化四未年ヨリ先拾ヶ年、所中ハ勿論、谷山・喜入・指宿・山川・頴娃・知覽・鹿籠百姓・野町互之縁與被成御免候事

37 市來江口濱・赤崎浦・神之川浦之儀、脱躰勞浦ニテ相當之縁與不相調、依願弘化二巳年より先キ拾ヶ年、所中百姓互之縁與被成御免旨被仰渡候事

38 頴娃諸浦相勞、依願文政八酉年ヨリ先拾ヶ年、所中井近鄕知覽・鹿籠・川邊・川

邊郡山田・喜入・指宿・山川・今和泉百姓・野町互之縁與被成御免候處、年限筈
合、又々天保八酉年ヨリ先貳拾ケ年、以前之通被成御免候事

事

39　知覽門之浦・松ヶ浦・西鹽屋浦・東鹽屋浦、別テ致困窮浦中互之縁與不相調、依
　　願文政元寅年以來拾ケ年ツツ及兩度、所中ハ勿論近鄕穎娃・川邊・川邊郡山田・
　　鹿籠百姓互之縁與被仰付置候處、年限筈合、又々依願嘉永元申年ヨリ先拾ケ年、
　　所中ハ勿論近鄕穎娃・川邊・川邊郡山田・鹿籠・加世田百姓互之縁與被成御免候

40　國分濱之市町之儀、由緒之以御取譯、年行司首尾能相勤候者退役後幷名頭家督之
　　者迄名字附被成御免候、且、名頭二男三男別立御奉公相勤候者又ハ以前屋敷致所
　　持當分無屋敷之者モ名頭と相唱來由候得共、名頭之名目ハ切坪ニテモ現ニ屋敷致
　　所持候者共迄ニ候条、以來紛敷無之樣可申渡旨、享和元年酉九月被仰渡候事

41　高山波見浦之儀、少人數ニテ浦並御奉公相勤來候得共、極貧者共ニテ他浦エ相掛
　　緣與難相調、依願所中幷近鄕野町・百姓互之縁與、文政十三寅年ヨリ先キ拾ケ年

被成御免候處、年限筈合、又々弘化二巳年ヨリ先キ拾ヶ年、以前之通被成御免候
事

42 串良柏原浦相勞、相當之縁與不相調、依願所中幷高山・大崎野町・百姓、來戌年
より先拾ヶ年、入縁被成御免候旨、天保八年酉八月十三日被仰渡候事

43 國分濱村浦之儀、往古由緒之御取譯を以、辨指首尾能相勤候者迄退役後・浦名頭
家督之者迄、名字付被成御免候旨、天保四年巳二月被仰渡候事

44 伊集院神之川浦之儀極々相勞、殊人少之場所ニテ相當縁與不相調、依願弘化二巳
年ヨリ先キ拾ヶ年、所中幷日置・市來百姓互之縁與被成御免候事

45 加世田大崎浦之儀、勞浦ニテ相當之縁與不相調、依願所中幷水引・谷山百姓互之
縁與、弘化三午年ヨリ先三ヶ年御免被仰付置候處、嘉永元申年迄ニテ年限筈合候
事

十七　諸人家内札幷御咎目者之親族又ハ缺落者改様之事

1　士幷郷士之外名字相名乗格式之者、親類之内何そニ付家内入之願申出候節、由緒
有之者ハ時々吟味之上家内入差免、手札帳面共ニ名字附ニテ可被差置候、以前ヨ
リ由緒無之之家内札ニテ罷居候者ハ、有來通無名字ニテ可被差置候、以來共ニ格式
不相知者ハ、其親類家内ニ片付都テ可爲無名字事
　但、無名字之者、諸人年季抱ニ出候儀ハ不苦、名字相名乗候格式之者ヱ養子之
　取組等紛敷儀も可有之候間、本何某家内ト手札帳面共ニ片書可致置候、右之娘
　類縁與之儀、諸人下人之娘縁與ニ準、外之者ヱハ取組之儀御免無之候

2　諸士幷郷士御咎目者又ハ缺落者、本人之儀ハ士被召放、右家内罷居候者與帳・高
帳被相除親類家内ニ被召入候者ハ、養子・別立其外御奉公方等不被仰付候、右
格式何様共不相究者候得ハ名字相名乗候儀ハ勝手次第候条、名字附ニテ致年附、
手札帳面等ニ本何某親類ト片書可有之事
　但、何方ニテモ下人下女ニ召仕候者、家部元證文ニテ召抱候儀ハ不苦候、永代

手札相直候儀堅御禁止之事候、尤、抱内格式之儀ハ抱主人可爲勝手次第候、右

娘類士幷郷士ェ縁與ハ御免無之候

3 與力以下之者名字相乗候者、前条同斷御咎目ニテ家内罷居候者共親族御當ニ付、

夫々之格式被召放候者ハ親類家内札ニ召入、無名字ニテ手札帳面共ニ本何某親類

と肩書ニ可有之事

但、右之者諸人下人同前之事候間、名字相乗候者ェ養子・縁與取與等之儀、

一切御免無之候

4 御咎目被仰付候者之跡家内親類ェ御預之者ハ、脇方ェ相除間敷事

但、無據依譯ハ、願之上預可相替候

5 士幷郷士致缺落缺戻リ候者ハ、遂披露於無子細ハ、無名字ニテ親類家内ニ可入置

事

6 缺落歸參者手札申請候ハ、何年何月何某を以歸參候段遂披露候由、法様之書附を

以札改奉行所エ可申出事

但、歸參者、札之面帳面ニモ缺落歸參・他國出禁止と可相記候

7　缺落者ハ、何年何月何某を以遂披露候由、家內改帳ニ書載、手札可取揚事

8　士被召放候者、本人遠島御赦免無之內、妻子幷家內之人數ハ親類御預雖爲御免、

此者共ハ親類之家內ニテ手札可爲取事

但、遠嶋被仰付候者之妻子、親類御預御免以後ハ、子共成行之格ニ應手札可爲

取候

十八　上方抱者幷御國居付者類改様之事

1　上方年季者・居附者・永代者幷他國者御國エ居附候男女共、初テ手札取候者ハ、

年季座可爲證文事

但、年季・居附・永代之譯、本國・何方何某抱と札之肩書可相記候

2 右之者共幷古永代者從前々手札取來候者、如古札可爲取事

3 上方永代抱者之儀ハ、抱主人親子兄弟之外ニハ札元相直候儀不罷成御法ニテ候處、御國居付者之儀ハ勝手次第抱主人相直事候間、上方永代者モ居附者同前相對相除候儀被成御免候旨、安永四年未十月被仰渡候事

4 年季明上方ヨリ請取人無之者居附願候ハ、抱主ヨリ年季座ヱ可申出候、不片附內八年季座以證文手札可申請事

　但、以後片付手札相渡候節ハ、年季座可爲證文候

5 上方抱者、死失又八年季明罷登候者、惣テ家內改帳ニ書載、手札可取揚事

6 上方永代抱者、依科諸所百姓下人ニ被下候者、本抱主人之名前手札帳面共永々可書記置候、尤、當主人之名前モ手札帳面ニ可書記事

7　問屋附稼證文之旅人子致出生候ハ、其譯、法樣之書物を以札改奉行所ェ申出可相
究事

8　御國居付者之女、御當地町人女同前緣與出入被成御免候間、町奉行・御舟奉行・
主人證文を以手札可相直事

9　金山根帳附之者、諸士又ハ家中者永代召抱候節ハ、金山奉行より御勝手方ェ申出
御免許之上相抱事候間、向後札改奉行所不及證文、金山奉行證文ニテ手札可相直
事
　但、諸人永代召抱候節ハ、至子孫候テモ、本國幷金山根帳付之譯肩書可相記候

10　山ケ野・鹿籠兩金山居住之山師共、當時根帳付之者無之、人家來而已ニテ山稼方
差支候儀有之候付、是迄人家來之分ハ都テ此節身分被相替、金山山師之名目ニテ
金山奉行所付被仰付、身分格式之儀、物奉行所付同樣手札帳面共ニ名字付ニテ致
年附、本國幷金山根帳付之譯肩書ニ相記候樣被仰付、足輕以下緣與御免被仰付候、
左候テ諸鄉鄉士モ中宿ニテ致金職居候付、職內金山奉行支配被仰付、其鄉之諸役・

出銀等被成御免、何事モ金山方ヱ相付候様被仰付候、以來諸國より爲稼方入來候
者ハ、根帳付ニテ被召置候、且、谷山錫山之儀も諸事金山同樣被仰付候旨、文政
三年辰三月被仰渡候事

11 金山奉行所附山ヶ野金山居住者共、少人數ニテ相當之緣與難調、依願天保十二丑
年より貳拾ヶ年、横川・本城・湯之尾・馬越・曾木・溝邊・栗野・踊鄉士以下互
之緣與被成御免候旨、天保十二年丑正月被仰渡候事

12 右同斷鹿籠金山居住者共、少人數ニテ相當之緣與難調、依願天保十二丑年より貳
拾ヶ年、加世田・坊泊・川邊郡山田・川邊・久志秋目・阿多鄉士以下互之緣與被
成御免候旨、天保十二年丑正月被仰渡候事

13 右同斷谷山錫山居住者共、少人數ニテ相當之緣與難調、依願天保十二丑年ヨリ貳
拾ヶ年、谷山・伊作・田布施・阿多・川邊鄉士以下互之緣與被成御免候旨、天保
十二年丑正月被仰付候事

十九　公義流人幷他國者改樣之事

1 公義流人初テ札取候者ハ、預主ェ取次、御用人より之證文見屆、手札可相渡候事

但、本國何方何某預と手札可致肩書、御預替之節モ御用人證文見屆手札可相直候

2 流人御赦免、或死失、或缺落者等手札取揚候節モ、御用人證文を以可取揚事

3 他國者、數年御國ェ罷居諸郷方々致徘徊手札不申請者於有之ハ、詮儀之上、何國之者何年より參居候段、其所之郷士年寄・役人ェ委細相糺、札改奉行所ェ可申出之事

二十　御勘氣者幷窄舍者・遠嶋人改樣之事

1 依御勘氣士・郷士幷足輕・御小人・御口之者・御數寄屋仕坊主被召放候者手札之

儀ハ、親類之家内又ハ何方ニテモ其身望次第可爲取候、手札之面・帳内迄名字相除年附可致候、尤、妻子又ハ其者之家内人數迄可爲同斷事

但、右躰之者ハ、其家内ニ可入置者ヨリ、法様之書物を以札改奉行所エ可申出候

2 諸士幷郷士遠嶋被仰付候者之跡家内之儀、親類家内ニ不及召入候条、跡々之通ニテ手札可申請事

但、座附者・人家來・社家・寺門前・百姓・浦濱・町人等遠嶋被仰付候者、親族無御構由被仰渡候ハ、右ニ準帳面相調手札可申請候

3 遠嶋人幷依願嶋方居住之者ハ、何年何月何某を以被仰渡候由、家内改帳ニ書載手札可取揚事

4 遠嶋被仰付候者共ハ、於配所之嶋手札申請事候間、古札可取揚之事

但、士被召放遠嶋被仰付候者ハ、札之面名字相除、年附可相記候、士不被召放者ハ本之姿ニ名字可相記候

5　遠嶋人・依願嶋方居住之者、御赦免ニテ手札申請候者ハ、何年何月何某を以御赦免被仰付候由、法樣之書附を以札改奉行所エ可申出候

但、遠嶋ニテ申請候古札可差出候

6　遠嶋幷依願嶋方居住之者、於嶋元手札申請置、赦免之節不案内ニテ右手札不持登五ケ年迄手札不差出者ハ、不念ニテ差扣申出科錢三百文申付、新札之儀ハ札改奉行所エ間ニハ御勘定所エ扣置、嶋札差出候節引替可相渡旨、寬政十二年申四月被仰渡候事

7　遠嶋御赦免、又ハ出牢被仰付候者ハ、手札之面ハ其者共成行之格ニ應し可相記事

8　牢込之者何分と成行仰渡無之者ハ、親類方ニテ手札取置可申候、尤、右妻子家内人數モ親類より手札可爲取事

但、親類無之者ハ、其者支配之方より手札爲取候樣可致候

9　士幷鄉士依科牢込被仰付置候者之娘、脇方エ致緣與居初テ手札相直候者有之、本

人片付方不被仰渡內ニテ候ハ、手札取方之儀可得差圖事

10依科遠嶋被仰付置候者手札幷家內手札橫目切封ニテ親類エ預置候、手札之儀ハ、封之儘檢使方エ差出事候間、每之通可致改方候、且又、身分不被召放依科親類預リ被仰付置候者、親類不及家內入、以前之通手札可相渡候、尤、身分被召放親類預リ被仰付置候者ハ、是迄之通親類家內入、筋々エ相付願申出候樣可申渡旨、天保九年戌八月被仰渡候事

二十一 萬手札一卷見合方之事

1 紛失札・燒失札・盜札・男女違之儀、能々念入可相改之、於無別条ハ其趣證文見屆新札可出、紛失札又ハ男女違之儀ハ不念之事候間、先規之通科料可申附候、其外札之面を削、又ハ文字を書直、或似札・替札等、惣テ手札致聊爾候者於有之ハ、其子細承屆可有披露事

2　手札質物等ニ遣置置互之入與ニ付支ニ成候間、縦内々何様之譯有之候共、札元ェ相
返新札不申請候テ不叶事候間、札元ェ可相返候、若新札申請候以後預主ェ手札不
相返附人有之候ハハ、預方より其旨札改奉行所ェ可申出事

3　新札相調候刻、文字書違少々削書直候儀、向後障ニ罷成候間、右躰之節ハ札之面
惣様可書改事

4　古札・古帳引合相濟候節、古札ハ消候テ改檢使より銘々相渡、自分ニ白ケ候テ可
差出之、若薄札ハ調直候様可申渡事

但、諸人死人之儀ハ別紙ニ書記可差出候

5　如先改五人與帳前書、宗門改之趣書記、銘々判形を取、別册致可差出事

6　人數出入之證文互ニ可取直旨先達テ申渡置候間、差出候帳内證文引合於無相違ハ
帳面之上ニテ則可致淸書候、相違無之處ニ帳面相直候儀ハ改之日數相增之間、無
子細儀ニ隙不取様ニ可致候、尤、一手ニテ何ケ所モ相改事候間、一郷を幾日ニ仕

舞候譯書記、札改奉行所ェ可差出之、若不相應ニ日數込候ハヽ、屹可及沙汰事

但、內改之日數可書出候

7 手札改無滯相濟候樣ニ先達テ申渡置候間、出入之證文若於相滯ハ、改檢使より札
改奉行ェ可得差圖事

8 手札年號月日・其者之名・年附、又ハ主人有之者ハ主人之名、其外町・在鄕・何
町何村之何左衞門抔と樒ニ可書記事

9 帳面幷手札之面、名書之上、何宗旨樒ニ可相記之、出生子之儀ハ、父母之宗旨を
以同前可書記事

10 此節之改ニ相洩手札不申請者ハ、改以後可相知事候間、則可申出之、若隱置脇方
より於露顯ハ、其者之主人又ハ支配頭、鄕ハ鄕士年寄・役人可爲越度事

11 札元出入後日除先御問附之儀も可有之候条、落札無之樣入念可相改之、就中段々

次證文ニテ新札申請候者、又ハ揚札ニ罷成候者、當主人方帳面巳年札元何某ト書

記筈候条、右躰之出入入念可相糺事

二十二　科料申附法様一卷之事

1　札之面前一向宗と肩書有之候を削捨候者、科銀可爲壹枚、且又一向宗肩書有之所^{ハ脱カ}

改人可致印形置候、尤、文字不消様入念可致所持旨可申聞事

2　手札取後候者、一改科錢壹貫文ッッ可申附事

3　琉球幷諸島ヱ渡海之節、難舩ニテ手札捨候者、上國之上於無相違ハ不及科錢、然

共罷歸其涯何分不申出候テ三拾六ヶ月相過屆申出候者ヱハ、科錢五百文可申附旨、

文政七申九月被仰渡候事

4　手札失候者、證據於有之八、科錢貳百文可申附候、證據於無之八、科錢可爲五百

文事

　但、手札盗ニ逢候者・男女違之手札取候者、科錢可爲五百文候

5　手札面蟲附ニテ文字分兼、又ハシみ附等ニて同斷之節八、科錢三百文申附、手札

取揚別段證文差出候樣、文化十二亥四月被仰渡候事

6　火災其外不意之災ニテ手札捨候者、科錢可爲五百文事

　但、證據有之者八、科錢申附間敷候、乍然其後届不申出拾貳ケ月相過届於申出

　八、科錢五百文可申付旨、文政七年申九月被仰渡候事

7　養ひ子を直子札申受候者、科錢可爲貳貫文事

　但、右實父、科錢五百文可申附候

8　科錢貳百五拾文宛

　右、郷士幷私領之者共與中ェ不念之儀有之候節八、組中與頭（脱カ）、町八年寄・年行司・

名頭、在郷ハ庄屋・名主・與中、其外寺門前・浦濱右ニ可準事

但、郷ハ郷士年寄・與頭幷郷士、私領ハ役人、逼塞・遠慮等之御咎目之節、科

銀可被仰付旨、戌三月被仰付置候得共、札改方之儀ハ科錢ニ被仰付候

9　百姓・町人・浦濱人・寺門前者之娘、借銀利錢之方ェ內々ニテ召仕候儀御禁止候、

若利錢之方幷爲日雇召仕置、自然出生之子於有之ハ、母方ェ可相附之、右躰之儀

ハ御法様違候条、兩親ェ科錢壹貫文宛可申附事

但、百姓・町人・浦濱人・寺門前之者を內內ニテ致日雇置、諸士之下女ェ取合

子共致出生候ハ、出生之子父方ェ可相附候、右式之儀ハ御法様違候間、兩親ェ

科錢可爲右同斷候

10　百姓・野町・浦濱人幷寺門前者娘、免證文なしニ召仕置、子出生候ハ、兩親ェ科

錢壹貫文宛たるへき事

11　百姓之子、御法様違之者內々致養子候者、兩親共科錢可爲貳貫文事

但、右之子百姓ェ可返附候

12
百姓幷野町之者手札質物ニ遣置候ハ、科井杭可為七拾本事

13 科井杭五十本宛

右ニ付、掛合幷五人與ェ、右之通科物可申付之事

14 科井杭七拾本

右ニ付、野町年行司又ハ部當之内、右之譯存候者ェハ、當人同前右之通科物可申付之事

15 科錢三百文

右ニ付、百姓外之者掛合相立候者ェハ、右員數科錢可申附之事

但、質物ニ遣候譯存候庄屋幷部當役、郷士ヨリ相勤候者ェハ科錢申附筈候間、可得差圖候、右之譯不存庄屋・年行司・部當ェハ、御構無之候

16 科井杭百五拾本

右、百姓幷野町之者年季筈合候以後本門ェ不相返、内々ニテ召置、子共致出生

候者エ、右之通科物可申付之、尤、庄屋・部當咎目之儀ハ、可爲右同斷事

17　科井杭百本宛
　右之譯ニ付、與中エ右之員數科物可申附之事

18　慶賀并穢多村之者エ百姓致縁與候者、双方共科銀可爲壹枚ツ丶事

19　手札改ニ付何そ不調法有之候節ハ、士并鄕士・寺持出家ニテも、夫々相當之科錢
可被仰付候事

20　手札之面削捨候又ハ書改候者、縱不案內・幼少たりといふとも、科銀壹枚、自然幼
少者不調法之節ハ、親・兄弟・親類抔之內引受居候者ヨリ科銀可出事

21　手札之面輕き文字少々之書違ハ御咎目ニ不及候得共、多人數之書違又ハ年附・肩
書等之類書違候ハ、書役之儀ハ勿論改方エ相掛候役々、御咎目可被仰付事

二十三　雜

1　琉球幷諸島ェ渡海之者、手札持參致し古札無之旨申出者於有之ハ、能々承究、別条
於無之ハ改所ェ新札致格護置、其者罷歸候節、古札取揚新札可相渡候、札改奉行
所相仕舞候以後ハ、古札御勘定所ェ差出新札相渡候届可申出事

但、右躰之者別册書拔、札改奉行所ェ可差出候

2　諸人養ひ子之内、不審成札之取樣於有之ハ、能々承届子細無之者ハ、前々之通手
札可爲取事

3　養ひ子之儀、養子之文字ニ紛敷有之候間、養ひ子とひ之字を付相認候樣、文政四
年巳五月被仰渡候事

4　足輕・御口之者・御小人・御數寄屋仕坊主・百姓・野町・浦濱人・社家・寺門前・
士之家來下人等ニ至迄、生子紛敷者モ可有之候間、父母相糺直子無別条段承究、

惣テ先改以後生子不洩様入念相改新札可爲取候、他行之者ェも手札可出之事

但、片親支配違又ハ主人違候ハ、銘々其譯、證文可見届候

5　譜代之家來・下人ニテ無之者を、分限不相應ニ家内札取直、多人數方々ェ差置候
儀、町・在郷之妨ニ成候ニ付、前々ヨリ御禁止之事候条、不相應手札申請請人於
有之ハ、札改奉行所ェ可得差圖事

6　手札改相濟新札可相渡刻、諸人男之分ハ自身罷出可請取之、就中百姓・町人・浦
濱人男之分ハ惣様召出、先規之通銘々見届手札可相渡事

7　何方之支配ニモ不相附者於有之ハ、百姓ニ被召成御法ニ候、右躰之者於有之ハ可
有披露事

但、此以前ハ、右躰之者浮世人と相唱候間、入念可相改候

8　依科移者ニ被仰付置候者之娘、本在所ェ緣與爲致間敷事

九　缺落者幷他國者内々ニ抱置候儀、前々ヨリ御禁止之事候間、若密々隱置儀も可有
之候間、入念可相改之、尤、依時宜相搦捕之可有披露事

十　江戸定府・京・大坂居付之面々ハ、手札不及被仰付、宗門人數附帳迄を差出、札
改方エ致格護置、後年改之節帳内引合候樣可有之事

十一　士幷郷士末々ニ至迄男女共、無故行方不相知又ハ舟中ニテ舟不相見得數年何樣と
も不相片附者ハ、札改之節吟味次第手札取揚、萬一至後年ニ罷歸候者ハ、新札可
爲取事

十二　長崎居付之面々、京・大坂居付同樣手札不及被仰付、宗門人數附帳迄を差出候樣
被仰付候旨、弘化三年午九月被仰渡候事

十三　諸士依科、家來下人揚者ニ被仰付候節、申請之寄合以上ニハ御免無之御法ニ候、
且又右揚者闕當之者より以後脇方エ永代相直候儀、御免不被仰付事候、然とも申

請人相果主人無之節ハ、願之上脇方ェ相直候様ニ被仰付候事

14諸所ェ被召置候綱差家部被召立候ニ付、中間縁與迄ニテ難相調、百姓・町人等互
之縁與御免被仰付度旨、御鳥見頭ヨリ申出趣有之、百姓・町人互之縁與幷養子等
差越候儀御免被仰付候、尤、綱差等之儀ハ百姓ニテ、其家部嫡子代々綱差勤被仰
付其内末子ニテモ綱差職分勝テ御用立候者も有之候ハ、綱差ニモ可被仰付候得共、
先二男以下ハ百姓被召成、所役々見計を以申出、明合之田地ニテモ爲取百姓之家
業相勤、綱差家內ェ罷居候末子八年季奉公等出候節ハ、御鳥見頭ヨリ差免、百姓
相成候以後ハ、外百姓同様之仕向被仰付旨、寛政七年卯四月被仰渡候事

15屋久嶋・種子嶋ェ居住申付、又ハ爲折檻屋久嶋ェ遣置候者共儀、居住之所ニテ新
札申請候様被仰付候旨、文化十二年亥六月被仰渡候事

二十四　慶賀・穢多幷行脚者改様之事

1　慶賀・穢多・行脚之者手札可爲横印事

　但、直印取來候慶賀・穢多ハ先規之通可爲取之、慶賀・穢多下人之儀ハ可爲横

印候

2　男女共行脚罷成候者其家内相除候者ハ、近所之證據書差出、支配有之者ハ支配頭

以證文札元可相除事

3　諸所ェ致徘徊候非人共之内ェ、俗生等不相知物貫躰ニテ致渡世無札者紛居候儀も

可有之、何方之支配ニモ不相附者ハ百姓ニ被召成御法ニ候得共、乞食躰之者ニテ

百姓被召成候テも其詮無之者ハ、吟味之上、其所之穢多より手札申請候様、文政

三年辰十月被仰渡候事

4　飯野上江村之内穢多名頭藤元彦六事、先祖代格別成御奉公爲相勤譯合ニ付、藤元

名字被下置候處、致中絶無名字罷成居、此節願出趣有之、別段之御取譯を以、嫡
々迄名字付幷手札竪印御免被仰付候旨、天保十一年子十二月被仰渡候事

右條々堅固相守之札改可入念、右之外各難及了簡儀ハ、幾度モ札改奉行所ヱ可
得差圖、郷・私領之儀ハ郷士年寄・役人ェ申談可相改ハ、若大形之儀於有之ハ・
可及沙汰之條、緩之儀有間敷者也

　　　　　　　　　　　　　　　　　　　　　　　　　　札改奉行

　　　　　　　　　　　　　　　　　　　　　　　　　　　　新納內藏

　　　　　　　　　　　　　　　　　　　　　　　　　　　　北郷男吏

　　　　　　　　　　　　　　嘉永五年子正月

　　　　　　　　　　　　　　　　　　　本田六左衞門

　　　　　　　　　　　　　　　　　　　　　　穎娃織部